Harry
Houdini

Harry Houdini

Vicki Cobb

DK Publishing, Inc.

LONDON, NEW YORK, MUNICH,
MELBOURNE, AND DELHI

Editors : Jennifer Quasha, Elizabeth Hester
Publishing Director : Beth Sutinis
Editorial Assistant : John Searcy
Senior Designer : Tai Blanche
Art Director : Dirk Kaufman
Creative Director : Tina Vaughan
Photo Research : Anne Burns Images
Production : Ivor Parker
DTP Designer : Milos Orlovic

First American Edition, 2005

05 06 07 08 09 10 9 8 7 6 5 4 3 2 1
Published in the United States
by DK Publishing, Inc.
375 Hudson Street, New York, New York 10014

Published in Great Britain by Dorling Kindersley Limited.

Library of Congress Cataloging-in-Publication Data

Cobb, Vicki.
  Harry Houdini / by Vicki Cobb.-- 1st American ed.
    p. cm. -- (DK biography)
  Includes bibliographical references and index.
  ISBN-13: 978-0-7566-1245-0   ISBN-10: 0-7566-1245-4 (pb)
  ISBN-13: 978-0-7566-1246-7   ISBN-10: 0-7566-1246-2 (plc)
  1. Houdini, Harry, 1874-1926--Juvenile literature. 2. Magicians--
United States--Biography--Juvenile literature. 3. Escape artists--
United States--Biography--Juvenile literature. I. Title. II. Series.
  GV1545.H8C63 2005
  793.8'092--dc22

                        2005006995

Color reproduction by GRB Editrice, Italy
Printed and bound in China by
South China Printing Co., Ltd.

Photography credits:
Front cover: Corbis/Richard T. Nowitz; Back cover: Owaki -
Kulla/CORBIS; Half-title page: Richard T. Nowitz; Full-title page:
Will & Deni McIntyre/Corbis

Discover more at
www.dk.com

Contents

Failure Means a Drowning Death

"Ladies and gentlemen!" The elegantly-dressed magician hurled his voice out across the footlights. "I will now perform the best escape I have ever invented." The audience members glanced at each other expectantly. The Great Houdini was going to show them his latest and most dangerous death-defying feat yet. Up to this point in the evening he had entertained them with traditional magic tricks—cards and rabbits appearing and disappearing. His direct, confident manner and piercing gray-blue eyes had charmed and captivated them. But Harry Houdini was famous for his escapes, particularly from locks, chains, and handcuffs. The date was January 27, 1908, and he was on tour as usual, appearing in St. Louis, Missouri.

Houdini often used

Houdini dressed up in evening clothes for his performances. His wife often complained that he was rough on his clothing.

escapes to gain publicity for his performances. The day before the St. Louis show, he had appeared at the local police station. He had stripped off almost all his clothes and had been examined by a doctor to make sure he had no keys or lock picks hidden on his body. The police had then put several pair of handcuffs and leg irons on him and locked him in a cell. He was left alone, seemingly helpless— and then walked in the front door of the station, fully dressed, five minutes later. News of Houdini's police-station escape had guaranteed a packed house for this evening's performance.

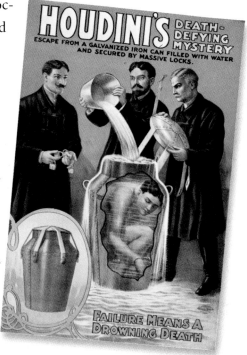

This poster promoted the milk-can escape. Houdini was 34 and at the height of his career when he introduced it.

Tonight he would unveil a spectacular new trick, never before seen in public. The audience moved closer to the edge of their seats. This, at last, was the grand finale they had all been waiting for.

Two men carried in a heavy iron can. It was shaped like the containers used by farmers to collect milk, only it was much larger—big enough to hold a man. Houdini banged on the can with his fist to show how solid it was. He invited several audience members to come on stage and inspect it for themselves. Its construction was simple—a solid metal body with a tapered collar riveted to it. There was only one way out—through the top. If there was a trap door or hatch or some other trick for escaping the can, no one could find it. The inspectors agreed that it was the real deal—definitely escape-proof.

Houdini left the stage for a minute, then returned wearing a bathing suit. He was a short man, only five feet five inches tall, but well-muscled, clearly an athlete. He explained that he would be handcuffed and locked in the can. To heighten the challenge, his assistants began filling the can with 22 pails of water. "A man can only live for a short time deprived of life-sustaining air," he reminded the audience (as if they needed to be reminded).

Handcuffs were locked around his wrists in front of him. He climbed into the can, splashing water onto the stage. As he sank down he said to the audience, "When you see me take a breath and submerge my body beneath the water just before the lid is locked on, I want all of you in the audience to draw that same breath. Hold it as long as you possibly can and when you are forced to let out that breath, at that point you would commence drowning." Just before he disappeared from view he added, "Should anything happen, and should I fail to appear within a certain time, my assistants will open the curtains, rush in, smash the milk can and do everything possible to save my life.… Music, Maestro, please!" The lid was then screwed on and locked with six padlocks. The assistants

Houdini squats in the milk can, about to be locked underwater by the local police. The six padlocks they will use are on the floor in front of the can.

9

A fire ax like this one was kept ready to rescue Houdini in case of an emergency and also to add to the drama of the moment.

placed a curtained screen around the can. The orchestra played a slow, mournful song called "Asleep in the Deep." Everyone knew the lyrics to the chorus:

> *Loudly the bell in the old tower rings,*
> *Bidding us list to the warning it brings:*
> *Sailor, take care! Sailor, take care!*
> *Danger is near thee, beware! Beware!*
> *Beware! Beware!*
> *Many brave hearts are asleep in the deep.*
> *So beware! Beware!*

Franz Kukol, Houdini's Austrian assistant, stood by the curtain holding a fire ax ready to smash open the can. Every five seconds Kukol announced the time elapsed. After a minute and a half, most people in the audience had already gasped for air. Three excruciating minutes ticked by. Anxiety buzzed through the theater. The audience had come to see Houdini face death, but no one wanted to actually witness him die. Just as

THE GREATEST ENTERTAINER OF ALL TIME

3 SHOWS I

Kukol moved toward the curtain, ax raised to strike, a breathless, soaking-wet, smiling, unshackled Houdini, bounded through the curtain, arms raised triumphantly. With a flourish he pulled back the screen to reveal the can behind him still padlocked. His water-filled prison was secure and seemingly untouched! The audience went wild—cheers, whistles, a standing ovation. Once again, Houdini had overcome seemingly insurmountable odds and escaped victoriously.

Houdini's intense and mesmerizing gaze captivated audiences. His smile, in contrast, was boyishly charming.

How did he do it? Was he a fake? Was he a master? Who was he? How did he become this extraordinary showman?

How did he become a legend—the greatest magician of all time, still talked about and written about more than 80 years after his death?

Houdini promoted himself as a "master mystifier." He felt that he was much more than just a magician.

11

chapter 1

The Weiss Family

Harry Houdini was born in Budapest, Hungary, on March 24, 1874, the third child of Rabbi Mayer Samuel Weiss and his second wife, Cecilia. They named him Ehrich. Rabbi Weiss had been a widower; his first wife died when she gave birth to the Rabbi's eldest son, Herman, in 1863. Harry Houdini liked to tell the story of how his parents met: It seems that a friend of Rabbi Weiss, who was shy and insecure, asked the rabbi to propose marriage for him to pretty, young Cecilia Steiner. The rabbi agreed. Upon meeting the young woman, he realized that the feelings of love that he expressed to her on the part of the young man were actually his own. Cecilia, for her part, preferred the rabbi to the absent suitor and married him despite the fact that he was 13 years older than she was and already had a child. Rabbi Weiss was 45 when Ehrich,

Cecilia Weiss, Houdini's mother, was one of the great loves of his life. Ehrich was her third son, one of five boys and one girl.

his fourth son, was born.

In 1876, at the age of 47, Rabbi Weiss left his home country, his pregnant wife, and four sons to immigrate to America to find a new home. What made him do it?

Over the centuries, Jews in Hungary went through periods of persecution for their religious beliefs. Even when they were tolerated, Jews were prevented from owning property and had to live in restricted areas. But this changed in the middle of the

Rabbi Mayer Samuel Weiss, shown here in his late forties, worked as a rabbi in Budapest.

nineteenth century. Most of the restrictions limiting Jews were abolished in Hungary by 1860, and Jews were allowed to enter all professions and live where they wanted. In 1869, a bill on Jewish emancipation was passed in Hungary's capitol, Budapest. This meant that Jews were considered full citizens both economically and socially. Jews who were persecuted in neighboring countries began to move to Budapest and

EMIGRATE

To emigrate is to leave a place, often a native country, to live in another country.

13

play an important role in the economic and cultural development of Hungary. This new opportunity for Jews to participate fully in Hungarian society led to a split among Jews and the creation of a new sect—Reform Judiasm. The religious practices of the conservative orthodox Jews prevented them from fully entering society, while reformed Jews could more freely participate in the cultural and business activities of the city.

Rabbi Weiss, however, failed to take advantage of opportunities in Hungary to support his growing family. Although he was a member of Reform Judaism, perhaps he still felt pressure from the more traditional Jews. He may have felt that he could not successfully compete with other rabbis and had a hard time making a living in Hungary.

Rabbi Weiss had a friend in Wisconsin who invited him to come to America. Perhaps the rabbi thought that eventually his family would be better off there. Whatever the reason, he made the journey, leaving his family behind, and settled in Appleton, Wisconsin. He took a job as the rabbi for a congregation of 15 Jewish families. In 1878, two years after he had left, he sent for his wife and his five sons. Theodore, later nicknamed "Dash," was the baby.

Unfortunately, Appleton did not live up to its promise of greener pastures for the Weiss family. After four years, Rabbi Weiss was out of a job. The Appleton congregation had replaced him with a younger man. Also, another son and a daughter had been born. Although he was well educated and spoke Hebrew, Hungarian, German, and Yiddish, Rabbi Weiss did not learn English. He probably seemed out of step to American Jews.

At age 53, Rabbi Weiss moved his wife and seven children to Milwaukee. However, he never got another job at a synagogue. He did what he could to make ends meet, moving the family from one small dwelling to another, conducting an occasional service and giving lessons. But the financial struggle never let up. At one point, Cecilia appealed to the Hebrew Relief Society for coal and groceries.

Ehrich, like many children of immigrants, wanted to leave the "old country" behind and become a true American. As an adult, he fabricated the story that he had been born on April 6, 1874, in

This photograph of Ehrich Weiss at age 3 ½ was taken just before he came to America.

Appleton, although there was a birth certificate for "Ehrich Weiss" with the March date back in Budapest. Because his family moved so much, Ehrich only attended school occasionally. Although he did learn to read and write, spelling poorly would become a life-long problem. Ehrich started earning money shining shoes and running errands at the tender age of eight. When he was 11, his older half-brother, Herman, who was only 22, died of tuberculosis, a contagious lung disease. This was Ehrich's first experience with death, and it had a profound effect on him. When Ehrich was 12, his father asked him to promise always to take care of his mother. Still unsuccessful in providing for his family, Rabbi Weiss had to turn to his children for help—a humbling reality for a father. Houdini later wrote, "…one morning my father awoke to find himself thrown upon the world, his long locks of hair having silvered in service with seven children to feed, without a position, and without any visible means of support." Ehrich would have to grow up fast. He had no other choice.

Ehrich ran away in the hopes of finding work elsewhere. He sent his mother a postcard: "I am going to Galveston,

Texas, and will be home in about a year. My best regards to all....Your truant son, Ehrich Weiss." Actually, he got on the wrong freight car and wound up in Kansas City, Missouri. For the next two years he worked odd jobs, moved around, and took care of himself as best he could, sending money home from time to time. One summer, a couple took him in and gave him a home for several months. Through it all, Ehrich stayed in touch with his family through letters. When he heard that his

Ehrich Weiss sent this postcard to his mother when he ran away at age 12. He signed it "Your truant son."

father had moved to New York City to look for work, Ehrich joined him there, and the two shared a room in a boarding house. The rest of the family came from Wisconsin after several months. They settled in an apartment with no hot water, where they could hear the rattle of the elevated trains through their window.

It was in New York that Ehrich began to study and practice the fascinating art of performing magic and opening locks.

chapter 2

Show Business in the 1890s

The entertainment business today is very different from the way it was when Ehrich Weiss was a boy. Today, a push of a button is all it takes to get professional shows and music in your home. But in the nineteenth century, entertainment was live. People had to plan ahead and leave their homes to find performances. Then, like today,

This poster advertised a circus that traveled by rail. For many, the circus was their introduction to show business.

Vaudeville

The word "vaudeville" comes from the French "Vau de Vire" which was a valley of the Vire River in France. Taverns in this area had a tradition of entertainment that included ballads and skits. The vaudeville era began in the 1880s with a theater in New York that was advertised as a "straight, clean variety show" suitable for families. Individual acts from a variety of cultural backgrounds, gave the audience something for everyone as cities were becoming increasingly crowded and diverse.

people still loved a good show. Every town in America had a theater, a church, or a barn for traveling entertainers passing through. Even open fields could become the scene for a show when a circus came to town and set up its tents.

The pinnacle of show business in the 1890s was called "vaudeville." All kinds of acts—musicians, singers, dancers, and comedians—appeared as a variety show in a theater. Posters advertising the event were plastered all over town. Newspapers featured the artists and reviewed the show. The top performers were paid well and became famous. Some of the biggest names included comedian Jack Benny and singers Sophie Tucker, Al Jolson, and Eddie Cantor. They worked hard, doing two shows a day, traveling

A vaudeville theater usually occupied a prominent position in the center of town. The booking agency occupied offices upstairs.

19

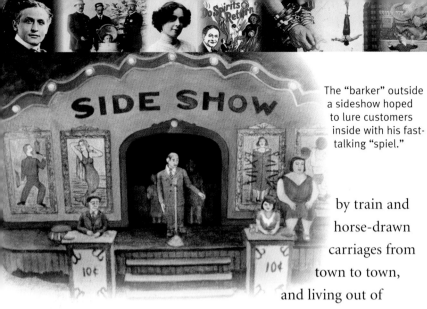

SIDE SHOW

The "barker" outside a sideshow hoped to lure customers inside with his fast-talking "spiel."

by train and horse-drawn carriages from town to town, and living out of suitcases. Despite these hardships, vaudeville was every performing artist's dream. It was the big time.

At the lowest end of show business were the "dime museums," where tiny stages were arranged beside each other, each displaying a different performer. The stages could be set up in storefronts, barns, or almost any kind of available building. Some of the performers were called "freaks" because they had a disability or looked unusual—for example, an armless man or a fat lady. In order to draw an audience, promoters put up huge posters, sometimes exaggerating the

The DOG-FACED MAN.

KOHL & MIDDLETON'S
South Side Dime Museum,
MONDAY, MARCH 2d.

Facial hair on the forehead made this man worthy of display as a freak in a dime museum.

descriptions and names of the attractions. The "Transparent Human Head," "Zulu Warriors," "Living Head Without a Body," "Turtle Boy," and the "Bewitching Albino Sisters Whose Flowing White Hair Reaches Below Their Waists" are some examples of the featured exhibits.

If the show didn't live up to its advance billing, no one seemed to mind. For example, the Transparent Human Head was actually a 19-month-old child with a lamp behind its head so the audience could see the silhouette of the baby's brain and blood vessels. Jugglers, strongmen, acrobats, and magicians performed as often as 20 times a day. The admission was one thin dime. Even then a dime was not much money. (That ticket today would cost about $2.20.) Once admitted to the show, visitors could walk around for as long as they wanted.

Another popular form of entertainment was a traveling medicine show, which was free. Medicine shows were produced by traveling salesmen who had

Jugglers performed in sideshows and dime museums as well as under the big top.

a "cure" to sell. The salesmen hired a performer to draw a crowd and then made their pitch to sell the product. Often the "medicine" (sometimes called "snake oil" or "worm killer") was of no value, but the idea of the show was to sell good times as much as good health.

For children, perhaps the most exciting day of the year was "circus day"—the day the circus came to town. Since it brought its own "theater" in the form of a tent, all a circus required was a big field. Months before, posters would be plastered all over town announcing the great event. On Circus Day, stores were closed and schools canceled classes. Special trains brought in spectators from outlying areas. People got up at dawn to watch the animals being fed and the tent, called the "big top," go up. Later in the day, crowds would line the street as the circus paraded to the big top. Camels, zebras, horses, marching bands, gilded-

In the 1890s, no other form of entertainment reached as many people as the circus. Circuses played rural areas as well as big cities.

A gilded circus wagon often held some of the animals used in the circus.

CONTORTIONIST

A contortionist performs bending feats by twisting his or her body into unnatural shapes, especially as entertainment.

cage wagons holding lions and tigers, and women in spangles riding elephants all added to the excitement.

No doubt Ehrich Weiss was in the crowd when the circus came to Appleton, Wisconsin. At age nine he created a little circus of his own with a friend and charged a nickel admission. He appeared as a contortionist (he could dislocate his shoulders, something he found useful later in life) and a trapeze artist, calling himself "Ehrich, Prince of Air." Later, he would claim that his act consisted of hanging upside down and picking up pins with his eyelids. A good story but probably not true.

Here, a contortionist balances on a strong man. Both are gripping a connecting shaft using their jaw muscles, which are among the strongest muscles in the body.

chapter 3

Learning a Trade

During the last 15 years of the nineteenth century, a massive influx of immigrants, primarily from Europe, came to America. Most of them passed through Ellis Island in New York Harbor. These immigrants provided a huge work force for many industries, including clothing manufacturing and railroads. The city of New York teemed with tenements—small apartments with no hot water, packed with families who struggled to make ends meet. Unfortunately, the opportunity for work was less than the demand, and many people lived in extreme poverty. Ehrich Weiss, however, proved to be a hard-working, resourceful teenager. He worked as a messenger boy and in a tool-and-die shop, where tools and metal cutting devices are made. He contributed

Ehrich Weiss wore this uniform as a messenger boy. In busy commercial city like New York in the 1890s, messenger boys could make good money, as telephones were scarce.

what he could to the family's needs. One cold December day he put his hat on the sidewalk and made a sign:

Christmas is coming
Turkeys are fat
Please drop a quarter
In the Messenger Boy's Hat

Passersby were amused by the charming young man and were generous. He took the coins he had collected and hid them all over his body—in his hair, up his sleeves, and behind his ears. When he got home he said to his mother, "Shake me, I'm magic!" When she did, coins scattered all over the floor to everyone's delight. Instead of simply turning over his windfall, Ehrich turned it into entertainment.

In 1888, when Ehrich was 14, he got a job by being creative and gutsy. He noticed a line of people outside a necktie manufacturer waiting to apply for a job as an assistant cutter. Ehrich realized he wouldn't stand a chance if he joined the line at the end. He walked up to the front, took the sign down, told the people in line that the job was filled, and went inside still holding the board. He was hired.

A full time job didn't leave Ehrich much time for school. But he did find time for athletics. He was an avid swimmer

25

and boxer and joined the newly formed Amateur Athletic Union in New York. He would run 10 miles a day to train for a race and won an AAU mile race in 1890 when he was 16, underage for the contest. When the officials realized he was too young, they took the prize away from him, but they eventually gave it back. Ehrich would not be denied any honor or medal he had worked for and earned, and he wasn't shy about wearing extra medals for the camera. Physical fitness became a way of life for Ehrich. As a teenager he vowed never to smoke or drink alcohol.

When a magician "palms" a coin, he appears to place the coin in the palm of one hand, but actually hides the coin in the other.

At the tie factory, Ehrich made a friend, Jake Hyman. Ehrich had become fascinated with magic and he shared that interest with Jake. Whenever they had a spare minute the boys practiced doing tricks.

Where did Ehrich learn the secrets of magic? Mostly from books. Despite the fact that he didn't attend school often, Ehrich's background encouraged him to value knowledge from books. The most respected people in a European Jewish community are rabbis and other scholars who spend most of their time reading. Ehrich had learned Hebrew and read the Torah to celebrate his Bar Mitzvah, or coming of age, at about 13, when he joined his father in New York. Ehrich knew how to use books to educate himself.

All "magic" tricks are really illusions. The first trick Ehrich mastered was the vanishing and reappearing coin. It involved making moves that distracted the observer so that the way the coin disappeared was not seen. If these moves were not done quickly and with confidence the trick would be obvious. Executing the illusion convincingly involved a lot of practice.

When Ehrich was 17 he read a book that changed his life. It was called *The Secrets of Prestidigitation and of Magic,* written by the

The Disappearing Spot

This trick is similar to Ehrich's first illusion. The audience initially sees an ink spot on both sides of the non-lighting end of a paper match. Then the magician blows on the match, and the spot disappears from both sides. This trick involves quick fingers, often called "sleight-of-hand" or "prestidigitation." How is it done? The magician makes two motions. One is large: the wrist of the hand holding the match turns back and forth apparently showing the observer the spot on both sides of the match. The second is small: while the wrist is rotating, the magician rubs together the thumb and index fingers very quickly so that the match flips over. The audience actually sees the same marked side. After blowing on the match, the same motions are made, showing the unmarked side.

famous French magician Jean Eugène Robert-Houdin (1805–1871). Not only did Robert-Houdin tell the secrets of his tricks but he also included the story of his life. He had been abandoned when he was young and was taken in by a magician who taught him to perform. After years of hardship he had become the greatest magician of his time, performing for royalty and living a luxurious life. Robert-Houdin became Ehrich's hero. Ehrich later wrote:

"My interest in conjuring and magic and my enthusiasm for Robert-Houdin came into existence simultaneously.... To my unsophisticated mind his 'Memoirs' gave the profession a dignity worth attaining at the cost of earnest, life-long effort. When it became necessary for me to take a stage-name, and a fellow-player [Jake Hyman] told me that if I would add the letter 'i' to Houdin's name, it would mean in the French language 'like Houdin,' I adopted the suggestion with enthusiasm."

A young Houdini examines the cuffs he's about to escape. Houdini said that even if he did the same escape that others did, the way he performed it made it fresh and interesting.

As it is today, it was common for people in show business to change their names to something distinctive and recognizable to the public. At home Ehrich's nickname was "Ehrie," and "Harry" was probably an Americanized version. So "Harry Houdini" became the new and lifelong identity of the immigrant son, Ehrich Weiss. In 1891, Ehrich and Jake left the tie factory to begin performing as magicians. They called

Jean Eugène Robert-Houdin was Houdini's idol, inspiring the beginning of his career.

themselves "The Modern Monarchs of Mystery." They left with the blessings of their boss, who wrote a letter of reference for Ehrich:

To Whom It May Concern:
We hereby certify that Mr. Ehrich Weiss has been in our employ for two years and six months as assistant lining cutter and we cheerfully recommend him as an honest and industrious young man.

Harry Houdini had embarked on his chosen profession, and it was not cutting fabric.

"Dime Museum Harry"

In 1892, Ehrich's father died, leaving Cecilia and her six children: Nathan, 22; William, 20; Ehrich, 18; Theo, or "Dash," 16; Leo, 13; and Gladys, 10. That same year, Ehrich launched his career as "Harry Houdini." He and Jake Hyman played at the dime museums and fairs around the northeast and midwest, calling their act "The Brothers Houdini" or "The Modern Monarchs of Mystery." In 1894, Jake went off on his own and Harry's real brother, Theo, joined his act. They performed card tricks, made flowers suddenly appear in empty lapel buttonholes, and produced handkerchiefs from a candle flame. The grand finale involved a large trunk with a trick escape hatch that they had bought for about $25, a huge investment at the time—especially when they were paid less than a dollar a show. But even though they paid for the apparatus they needed to do the trick and the secret to doing it, the way they per-formed it

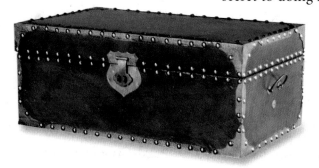

This steamer trunk is typical of the ones used in Metamorphosis: sturdy and seemingly escape-proof.

was unique. This escape became the first of Harry's trademark illusions.

Harry called their grand finale "Metamorphosis," which means "change in appearance." Harry would tie Theo's hands behind his back with a rope, then put him in a sack and tie the top. The tied and bagged Theo was then placed into the trunk which was locked and tied with ropes. A curtain was drawn so that no one could see the trunk, although they

This poster advertised Harry's signature act. Like many publicity posters, it contains bold claims—including the description of Metamorphosis as the greatest act of its kind in the world.

could hear Theo banging around inside. With great drama, Houdini told the audience, "When I clap my hands three times—behold a miracle!" He moved behind the curtain, clapped three times, and out stepped Theo, arms raised triumphantly. Theo then pulled back the curtain to show the trunk still tied and locked. He opened the trunk to reveal Harry inside, bagged and tied as Theo had been.

How did they do it? As soon as the top of the trunk was closed, Theo freed himself from the rope on his wrists and

Here is Bess in her twenties. In addition to helping Harry, she also worked as a singing clown.

cut a slit in the bottom of the bag. A trap door on the side of the trunk, near the bottom, allowed him to squeeze out past the ropes. Then Harry would crawl in to take his place. When the trunk was opened, Harry climbed out of the top of the bag and no one ever saw the slit. But even knowing how the trick is done, it is amazing that they could pull it off so quickly. It had to be practiced over and over so that every move was exactly right, in order to make the substitution possible in three seconds. Houdini kept his trunk trick as a part of his act for the rest of his career, although he changed aspects of it to keep it fresh. For example, he sometimes changed the patter around the trick, replaced the ropes around his wrists with handcuffs, or put chains around the trunk instead of ropes.

Harry tried everything to make a name for himself, including traditional card tricks. Some said that his technique with cards was not as advanced as his escape skills.

The brothers took jobs wherever they could—beer halls, local fairs, and small theaters. After deducting money for living and traveling expenses, they each kept only two dollars a week for spending money, and sent the rest home to their mother.

In the spring of 1894, the brothers were performing at New York's Coney Island. A pretty, petite eighteen-year-old girl, Wilhelmina Beatrice

Coney Island

Coney Island is a thin strip of land on the Atlantic Ocean at the mouth of New York Harbor. It reached its heyday in the 1890s when developers created amusement parks with rides and other attractions. A beautiful white sand beach made Coney Island a mecca for both rich and poor.

Rahner, was also performing there with a song-and-dance group called "The Floral Sisters." Harry fell madly in love, pursued her, and married her on June 22, 1894, three weeks after they met. "Bess," as Harry called her, was Catholic, but Harry's mother Cecilia had no trouble accepting her new daughter-in-law. On the other hand, Bess's mother didn't accept Harry's Jewish background until he and Bess had been married for twelve years. The 94-pound Bess was much better at getting out of the trunk than Theo, so she replaced him in the act, and the Houdinis hit the road together.

Houdini's Height

Harry Houdini was very sensitive about his height. Other magicians of his day, like Harry Kellar or Howard Thurston, were tall and imposing. Houdini gave his height as 5'5", but his passport listed him as 5'4." Bess's tiny size, at barely 5 feet tall was certainly one of her many attractions for him. He often stood on his toes when posing for pictures.

For the next six years, Harry and Bess performed at the lowest end of show business—dime museums, carnivals, small circuses, and tiny theaters. They sometimes did as many as 14 shows a day. They tried everything to become noticed and become a hit. They changed their name, temporarily appearing as the Rahners, Bess's maiden name. They did comedy, they sang, and Harry even tried hypnotism. The couple managed to save some money, but Harry invested it in a variety show and lost it. Sometimes Bess was so discouraged that she refused to appear with him. At the end of 1898 things were so bad that Harry later wrote, "I contemplated

"I contemplated quitting the show business, and retir[ing] to private life...."

–Harry Houdini

quitting the show business, and retir[ing] to private life, meaning to work by day at one of my trades…and open a school of magic." Their permanent home was with Harry's mother when they were in New York, which wasn't often.

But the tough years of "Dime Museum Harry" were not wasted. Houdini learned from every experience. Fourteen shows a day were excellent practice for the moves a magician must make to fool people. In a way, a magician is like a concert pianist. Sleight-of-hand requires dexterity

The Houdinis (front right) starred in the Welsh Brothers Circus in 1896.

of the hands and fingers and daily practice. Also, the incorrect English that he had learned on the street was refined. When a manager corrected his bad English—"Don't say, 'I ain't got nothing up my sleeve'"—Harry never said it again. He and Bess spent time with people who put on a variety of acts for audiences and Harry picked up skills from them. An armless man who played the violin with his feet taught Harry how to untie knots with his toes. A Japanese acrobat taught him how to swallow an ivory ball so that his mouth could be inspected and it would be empty. He could later regurgitate it whenever he wanted. At first Harry practiced this trick with a small piece of potato at the end of a string. The string helped him learn the moves needed to bring the potato back up. If he lost the potato down to his stomach, it was no big deal. After several weeks, he graduated to the ivory ball.

No doubt this technique helped Harry with another trademark trick he performed for the rest of his career. He would ask members of the audience to inspect his mouth to make certain there was nothing hidden inside. Then he placed a number of sewing needles in his mouth and began chewing

"Don't say, 'I ain't got nothing up my sleeve.'"

–A grammar lesson from one of Houdini's managers

them, claiming iron was good for the blood. Again his mouth was inspected and it was empty. The audience assumed he had swallowed the needles. Then he would appear to swallow a long knotted thread. When just the end of the thread was visible in his mouth, he slowly pulled it out. On the thread was the same number of needles he had "swallowed," each neatly separated from the other by a knot.

The one trade Houdini thought he could pursue if he gave up show business was that of a locksmith. There is a myth about Houdini (one of many) that he first became interested in locks when his mother locked up a pie in a kitchen cabinet when he was a young boy. Supposedly young Ehrich picked the lock to get the

Harry and Bess pose with the Metamorphosis trunk, shown tied with ropes. The bag used in the trick is at Harry's feet.

37

pie. Whether the story is true or not, there can be no question that Houdini was interested in the mechanics of locks. He collected them and he took them apart. In those days, locks were simpler than they are today, but Houdini never found a lock—a padlock,

A display showing some of the many handcuffs from which Houdini had escaped was put up in the lobby of the theaters where he performed his act.

a handcuff lock, a lock on a door—that he couldn't figure out how to open. His memory for all the different variations of locks was amazing. Even more extraordinary was his ability to have "a vision of the key." He could imagine the device that would open any given lock, and, once imagined, retrieve it from his extensive collection of keys and picks. In those years, he began to use handcuffs in his Metamorphosis routine instead of rope. He could open locks using keys, picks, and even by tapping on certain spots. All he needed was the right tool, and the lock was open.

How a Lock Works

A basic lock is a metal cylinder set inside a metal tube. A row of pins sticking down into the cylinder from the tube keeps the cylinder from turning when the lock is locked. Each pin is actually a pair of pins, one on top of the other. Although the lengths of each pair are equal, the break between each set come at different lengths. A key pushes up each pin so that the break lines up with the bottom of the tube, allowing the cylinder to turn. A lock pick also moves the pins but it takes skill to know when the pin is pushed up the right distance. Successful lock-picking depends on complete familiarity with the design of the lock.

Just before Harry was about to quit the stage to become a locksmith and a teacher of magic, he decided to give show business one last try. He had one last contract to fulfill.

He kept thinking that all he needed was one big break. He knew that he had paid his dues, so he was ready for that break when it came.

chapter 5

Martin Beck and "The King of Handcuffs"

In the early spring of 1899, Houdini was playing at the Palmgarten, a beer hall in St. Paul, Minnesota. A man in the audience with a thick German accent challenged Houdini to escape from a new pair of handcuffs, "perhaps more in a joke than sincerity," Harry later wrote. He and Bess had coffee with the man after the show. The man's concern was that the handcuffs not be "doctored" so that they could be opened by a trick. The next day the handcuffs arrived on stage. Harry was shackled in them and he quickly escaped. This impressed his challenger, who turned out to be the manager of the Orpheum circuit of theaters, a man named Martin Beck.

This famous photograph shows Houdini locked in handcuffs and leg irons. His rolled up sleeves to indicate that he had nothing to hide, but you can be sure there were lock picks somewhere handy.

Martin Beck, the legendary star-maker, had a theater named for him on Broadway in New York.

Martin Beck was a vaudeville tycoon—a star maker. Houdini saved the telegram he received from Beck on March 19, 1899: "You can open Omaha March twenty-sixth sixty dollars, will see act probably make you proposition for all next season." Harry wrote across the bottom, "This wire changed my whole Life's journey."

And change it, it did. Instead of the paltry $25 salary he was used to, Houdini started working for Beck at a salary of $60 per week, with a raise every few weeks. Within a few months he was earning $250 a week—the fee for headliners and top stars on the vaudeville circuit.

Martin Beck told Houdini to drop most of the magic tricks he was performing and to concentrate on handcuff

The Orpheum

The Orpheum Theaters were a chain of 16 theaters that extended from Chicago to San Francisco. They were known for classy and high-quality entertainment. The theaters were beautifully decorated, and their productions had the best costumes, props, music, and publicity. They also paid performers top dollar and required fewer shows from them. Orpheum's chief rival in the East was the Keith circuit. The two chains set the standard for the top shows in popular American entertainment.

escapes and Metamorphosis. Beck knew what he was talking about. Houdini had tried everything he could think of to reach his audience. He did all the usual tricks in a magician's repertoire. Beck's genius was to zero in on Harry's distinctive qualities and the abilities that set him apart from other magicians. With Beck's guidance, Harry discovered that less is more. Instead of bombarding an audience with one small trick after another, he concentrated on a few very creative and original feats and presented them with a dramatic flourish.

One way to emphasize that escaping handcuffs was a skill and not a "trick" was to invite the public to bring him their own handcuffs. This challenge was advertised on the posters announcing Houdini's appearances. At a typical performance, Houdini would invite audience members to come on stage with their manacles or handcuffs. (He had his own confederates or "ringers" in the audience in case no one stepped up.) The challengers would lock him up. Then he disappeared into

Houdini often posed for publicity photos wearing only chains. He was proud of his athletic physique.

his four-sided cabinet or "ghost house" as it was called. Within minutes he would emerge and throw open the cabinet, revealing all the shackles locked together in a chain.

Houdini only failed once. Sargeant Waldron of the Chicago police department locked Houdini up in his own special cuffs. Houdini struggled for more than an hour, with the audience getting more and more restless. At the end of the evening, Waldron confessed that he had stuck a small piece of lead in the lock to jam it. The doctored cuffs had to be sawed off. Fortunately, Houdini got good press for this fiasco. The *Chicago Journal* headline read: "Was an unfair test: Magician Houdini says Sergt. Waldron played a joke on him." But Houdini had learned his lesson. He never again put on a manacle or leg-iron without checking first to make sure the locks were in working order.

Inviting challenges to escape from handcuffs provided by audience members became a regular part of Houdini's act. It was a brilliant piece of showmanship because it emphasized that the manacles had not been tampered with

Ghost House

The "cabinet" or "ghost house" is a standard apparatus for magicians. Its purpose is to conceal the magician so that the audience cannot see how a trick is done. It can be a paneled screen or a booth with a door. It can be large enough for an elephant, although it is usually only big enough for a person. A panel may have curtains that can be drawn open or shut. The style of the cabinet depends on the trick being performed.

by either Houdini or the provider of the cuffs. It seemed like a fair contest. All Houdini needed was enough advanced warning to be prepared with the right device to open the cuffs. A selection of his most useful lock picks was often concealed in his ghost house, so escape was usually simple for Houdini. He learned that the show was more exciting if he didn't make the escape look too easy. Sometimes, after getting out of the handcuffs, he would sit in his cabinet reading a newspaper until the audience became nervous and antsy.

As Houdini and Bess traveled from town to town, Harry's reputation as "The King of Handcuffs" grew. In those days there was no national news media, only local newspapers and word of mouth. Harry had to create a newsworthy event in every town he played and make sure that reporters were there to see it. Typically he did this by dropping in on the local police and challenging them to lock him up in their most secure manacles and jail cell. A newspaper article in the *Omaha World-Herald* captured one scene:

Houdini's had a large collection of tools and lock picks. Some were for use in his act; others were just collectors items.

"The entire handcuffs and leg-irons of the police department were on exhibition and all of them were used that could be worn conveniently, or rather inconveniently....

The Bean Giant handcuffs were used in one of Houdini's most famous escapes. Notice how the position of the keyhole makes it impossible for the handcuffed person to reach it even if he had the key.

In less time considerably than it took to adjust this array of jail 'jewelry' he returned from an adjoining room, where it was impossible to conceal a confederate, relieved from the entire paraphernalia and having the same linked together, forming a chain."

In order to prove that he did not need a key to escape from jail, Houdini performed his escapes in the nude. He allowed himself to be examined by a police doctor who would verify that nothing was hidden on his body. After being shackled hand and foot, he would be carried, stark naked, into a cell. Of course, only men were present. However, many of Houdini's posters showed him handcuffed and naked. No doubt these images had shock value for the public—not a bad thing for someone seeking publicity as Houdini did.

Houdini lived during the Victorian era, a time of strict manners, high moral standards, and modesty. It is amazing

45

that Houdini's revealing photographs were not censored.
Indeed, they weren't even commented on.

In early 1900, one particularly stiff challenge came
from Captain Charles Bean, who had invented a number
of different kinds of handcuffs over the years—many of
which Houdini had escaped. Bean offered a $500 reward
to anyone who could escape from his Bean Giant handcuffs,
even giving the prisoner the key. Most handcuffs were rings
connected by a chain that allowed the prisoner to move
the hands and arms, but the Bean Giants were two bracelets
connected to a flat steel "box" containing the lock. The
keyhole was very small and impossible to reach when the
hands were locked in it. As the story goes, Harry said
to Captain Bean, "I have spread your fame for making
handcuffs all over the United States. I take

my hat off to your Yankee ingenuity." He was then locked into the Bean Giants behind his back. When he quickly reappeared, unfettered, Captain Bean said, "Well! Well! I couldn't believe it unless it took place before my eyes. I have probably fastened ten thousand prisoners in my time with those handcuffs, and have met with all sorts of experiences, but—you beat me!"

Perhaps more than any other event, Houdini's escape in March 1904 from the "Mirror" handcuffs made him the undisputed "King of Handcuffs" and "Master of Manacles." It happened several years after the Bean Giants, and after Houdini had become a star in Europe. He was appearing in London's Hippodrome, the newest and most spectacular theater in England. The challenge was issued by the *London Daily Illustrated Mirror.* Houdini was to escape a single pair of handcuffs made by blacksmith Nathaniel Hart who claimed that the lock on the cuffs "no mortal man could pick." The newspaper was full of descriptions and hype about the contest for five days leading up to the event.

The big day—March 17, St. Patrick's Day—finally arrived. The Hippodrome had an overflow crowd of 4,000 including more than one hundred reporters. The audience sat through a full variety program of six other acts, waiting impatiently for the main event. Finally, when Houdini appeared in his

London's Hippodrome was a state-of-the-art theater in its day. It was named for an arena in ancient Rome that could hold 250,000 people.

formal attire, he "received an ovation worthy of a monarch." He solemnly announced to the audience "I am ready to be manacled by the *Mirror* representative." The *Mirror* journalist came forward with the cuffs. He shook hands with Houdini, then called up a group of witnesses to make sure that the cuffing was fair. Houdini also had a group on stage to look after his interests. In total there were almost one hundred people lined up on the stage to act as referees.

The key was turned six times to lock him in. "I am now locked up in a handcuff that has taken a British mechanic five years to make. I do not know whether I am going to get out of it or not, but I can assure you I am going to do my best." The handcuffs looked truly escape-proof. With Bess

Houdini would repeat some of his escapes in his movie *The Grim Game*.

standing by, Harry entered his "ghost house" and the orchestra started playing. It was 3:15 in the afternoon.

This display placard was used for a theater lobby exhibit.

Twenty-two minutes later, Houdini stuck out his head. A cheer went up, "He is free! He is free!" some yelled, but it was a false alarm. He only wanted to get a better look at the lock in the bright stage lights. Back he went. Thirty-five minutes later he emerged again sweaty, his collar rumpled. "My knees hurt," he explained to the audience. A cushion was brought for him. He returned to his labors. Twenty minutes later he reappeared still handcuffed and looking exhausted. A groan went up in the audience. "Will you remove the handcuffs for a moment in order that I may take my coat off?" he asked.

Houdini designed this unique pair of handcuffs himself for use in his stage act.

The reporter said, "I cannot unlock those cuffs unless you admit you are defeated." Unflustered, Houdini removed a pen-knife from his pocket, turned his jacket inside out over

49

his head and shredded it off with the knife held between his teeth. The audience went wild and booed the *Mirror* representative for his decision. Houdini went back into his ghost house. Someone in the audience noted when an hour had passed. After 10 more minutes of anxious waiting Houdini bounded from the cabinet holding the locked handcuffs in his free hand. The newspaper wrote, "A mighty roar of gladness went up. Men waved their hats, shook hands one with the other. Ladies waved their handkerchiefs, and the committee, rushing forward as one man, shouldered Houdini and bore him in triumph round the arena. However, the strain had been too much for the 'Handcuff King' and he sobbed as though his heart would break."

The strain had been too much for Bess, as well. She had left the theater just before Houdini cut his coat off. But for Houdini it remained one of his greatest moments—the crowning event for the true "Handcuff King."

How did he free himself from all those shackles? Not easily. Harry himself said, "The path of a handcuff king is not all roses." If you asked him, he would always give a stock reply, "Please excuse me from answering. … If I were to do so my bread and butter would be gone." However, he made no secret that he had vast knowledge of locks and handcuffs. He instantly knew which of his many tools could

> *"My brain is the key that sets me free."*
>
> –Harry Houdini

Houdini collected handcuffs
so he could secretly substitute his
own cuffs if he didn't like the ones
brought by an audience member.

do the job, and if needed, he could invent a special device to help him. In the case of the Bean Giants he had created an extension that let him turn the key from a distance. His flexible body made it possible for him to bring back-manacled hands under his buttocks and legs to his front. His left hand could unlock his right hand as easily as the right could free the left, something he had practiced very hard to master. His ability with sleight-of-hand allowed him various ways of concealing a key or other tool. He could conceal a key or pick in a small metal case that he could swallow and regurgitate. He could hide his picks in his thick wavy hair or taped to the bottom of his foot. The particular way he did a trick was kept a secret from the public, although some books for magicians reveal the methods. Houdini knew that mystery only enhanced his reputation. So he would smile slyly and say, "My brain is the key that sets me free."

chapter 6

The "Self-Liberator" Conquers Europe

Handcuffs were not the only thing from which Houdini wanted to escape. At the end of his first tour of the Orpheum circuit in December of 1899, Harry was getting tired of Beck's management. Beck had been very "hands-on," writing Houdini often and giving him business and performance tips. He encouraged Harry to get a scrapbook for his reviews and to hold out for top pay. However, Houdini wanted to be independent and became irritated with Beck's direction. Beck took 20 percent of everything

The ship *Westernland* transported poor immigrants as well as first class passengers like the Houdinis.

Houdini earned, and Harry let him know that he resented it. Beck reminded him, "No manager would believe that your act was fit for vaudeville. They all considered it a museum act." By February they were both becoming annoyed with each other. Despite their conflicts, Beck booked Houdini to tour Europe during the summer of 1900.

In May, the Houdinis sailed for England.

In those days, there was only one way to get to Europe from America—by ship. A journey across the Atlantic lasted about 10 days, an eternity to Harry who was miserably seasick. Bess was so concerned that she tied Harry to his bunk when she had to leave the stateroom for fear he'd throw himself overboard. But Europe represented new worlds for the Houdinis to conquer. Several other American magicians had done well there, so Harry and Bess decided to take a chance.

Destination stickers from each of a traveler's stops were often plastered on luggage.

When Harry and Bess arrived in London they found that the promised bookings had fallen through. After a year of extraordinary success, they were suddenly without work. The agent they were supposed to meet with was out of town. But Harry Day, the agent's young assistant, was eager to help as a way of starting his own career in theatrical management.

The two Harrys took to each other right away. Day persuaded Duncan Slater, the manager of the Alhambra, one of London's premier theaters, to take a look at Houdini. Slater said he would give Houdini an audition, but only after he could prove that the handcuff escape was legitimate. A local escape artist, the Great Cirnoc, who also called himself the Handcuff King, always used his own manacles and the audience was not impressed. It was all too easy to "gaff" the cuffs so they could be easily opened. Harry would get an audition only if he could extricate himself from the handcuffs of Scotland Yard, London's most formidable prison. Of course, Harry agreed. In fact, he could hardly wait. On June 14, Day, Slater, and Houdini met with Superintendent Melville of Scotland Yard. Houdini's arms

The Alhambra theater featured the best acts in London.

were locked around a pillar with one of the Yard's regulation handcuffs. Day, Slater, and Melville began to walk out of the room, intending to leave Houdini to struggle for several hours. Before they had opened the door to leave, Harry called out for them to wait—he had already escaped. The audition was his, and Day became his permanent manager. Harry's only regret was that reporters hadn't been present.

This entranceway in London leads to Scotland Yard, a formidable prison considered in Houdini's day to be state-of-the-art in terms of restraining and punishing criminals.

However, that would be corrected at the audition. Only about 20 people attended the open audition in the Alhambra, which held 4,000, and they were mostly from the press. It was a bit of an insult for the magician who had been packing theaters all over America without having to audition. Nevertheless, Houdini appeared in full formal dress as if the hall were standing-room only. In the middle of his performance, a man climbed on stage claiming that he was the original Handcuff King and that Houdini was a fraud. It was none other than the Great Cirnoc, the man who used

Senator Chauncey Mitchell Depew vouched for Houdini during his Alhambra audition.

gaffed handcuffs, and whom Slater wouldn't book. A man in the audience stood up and said, "That is not true. I know that young man[Houdini]. … I saw him several years ago doing his handcuff act." He identified himself as Chauncey M. Depew, a U.S. Senator. Houdini got his chance.

Harry whispered to Bess, "Get me the Bean Giants." The contest was on. Cirnoc first insisted that Harry escape from the Bean Giants, which of course Harry did behind his cabinet, and quickly. Then Cirnoc was locked in the cuffs and given the key (which was useless, of course, since he couldn't reach the keyhole). Cirnoc had to admit defeat and the story made all the headlines the next day. Houdini began a sensational engagement at the Alhambra which launched his career in Europe. The Houdinis did not return to the United States for the bookings that Martin Beck had made for them later that year. In fact, they didn't return for any extended period during the next five years. Houdini's professional association with Martin Beck was over. They remained cordial with each other, but over the years, Harry gave Beck less and less credit for Beck's impact on his career.

Houdini added to his repertoire of escapes during his years in Europe. He was always thinking of ways to heighten the drama. In Germany, he was tied to a chair by sailors who, he explained to the audience, knew how to tie knots as part of their training. He did his escape in full view since there was nothing to conceal. Houdini simply used his amazing escape skills. "The whole secret is getting the first hand free; after that it is all plain sailing. The quickness with which one gets out depends on how much one can get a little slack in the rope. When I am about to be tied I always sit a little forward from the back of the chair; the people tying me do not notice this." As a last resort Houdini would expand his chest while being bound to give himself a little wiggle room later.

Metamorphosis remained a part of his act. The trunk was a bought prop,

> *"The whole secret is getting the first hand free; after that it is all plain sailing."*
>
> –Harry Houdini

Houdini fell on his side while struggling to escape the ropes. There was no trick here, and the audience appreciated his efforts.

rigged with a trap door by its manufacturer. But mystery was always added when a crate was constructed locally, provided by merchant from the town. So Houdini also added a packing crate escape. In every town he would get a wooden crate supplied by a local business. (The name of the supplier was often printed on the outside as free advertising.) After a committee of volunteers from the audience inspected the crate and vouched for its integrity, Houdini got inside. The lid was nailed into place by volunteers and bound by thick ropes. It was then enclosed in a large cabinet. The orchestra played its music softly so that the audience would be able to hear any banging. After 15 minutes, Houdini emerged without his jacket or shoes, his shirt-front wrinkled. Behind him the packing crate seemed untouched, still roped and nailed.

The secret, as usual, was in the preparation. When the packing crate was being constructed, Houdini depended on an assistant to be present. As Houdini himself put it, "He mingles among the committee as one of them and (unostentatiously) directs, assists, and steers the committee from placing too many nails in the part of the box that the performer intends to direct his attention to when imprisoned." As a result, a board on the side near the bottom was less securely nailed than the others. Houdini could use his exceptional strength to push out the board. There was, however, no limit to the number of nails put into the top since it played no part in the escape.

A securely nailed top only reassured the audience that escape was impossible.

When Houdini was touring in Halifax, Nova Scotia, in 1896, he was invited by a local doctor to visit an insane asylum. Houdini was fascinated with imprisonment of any kind, and the mentally ill often had to be locked up. Houdini had been very familiar with the restraints used on mental patients—muffs over the hands, belts, and bed straps. But on this visit he saw his first straitjacket and it became an unforgettable experience. "I saw a maniac struggling on the canvas padded floor, rolling about and straining

Here, Houdini is being restrained in a straitjacket. The sleeves have not yet been fastened behind his back.

59

Mental Illness

The treatment of the mentally ill was different in the 1890s than it is today. People who could not function in society were sent to institutions called asylums. Violent patients were restrained, often in a straightjacket, so that they would not be dangerous to others or themselves.

each and every muscle in a vain attempt...to free himself from his canvas restraint....I noted that were he able to dislocate his arm at the shoulder joint, he would have been able to cause his restraint to become slack in certain parts and so allow him to free his arms...this was the first time I saw a straitjacket and it left so vivid an impression on my mind that I hardly slept that night."

Houdini was determined to learn how to escape from a straightjacket, using his old trick of disclocating his shoulder. When the trick was mastered, it was added to the act. At first Houdini performed his escape behind the screen, emerging sweaty, disheveled, and dusty with torn clothing. However, the audience was skeptical that he had to work so hard. At the suggestion of his brother Theo,

This straitjacket from the 1890s is made of leather and canvas.

who was also an escape artist and magician known as Hardeen, Houdini began to perform the straitjacket escape in full view of the

audience. Full disclosure only heightened his growing fame and reputation. As a newspaper described it, "He wriggles and squirms" and "Humps and writhes, slips his head under his arm, skates along on one shoulder, chews a buckle or two and peels off his crazy house trappings as a boy does his bathing suit." Houdini was willing to do whatever it took to make a better show.

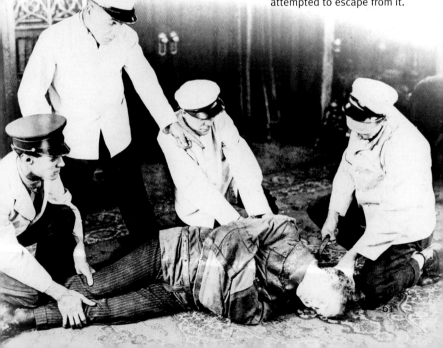

Authorities always checked a straitjacket before Houdini attempted to escape from it.

chapter 7

The Self-Promoter

In show business, money follows fame. No one understood this better than Harry Houdini. Early in his career, when he still privately called himself "Dime Museum Harry," he had advertised that he would escape handcuffs while tied to the back of a "wild" horse. But when Houdini began to wriggle on the horse's back, it got spooked and took off—finally stopping, exhausted, miles from the spectators. Houdini freed himself but only the horse saw him do it. The lesson: no matter how great the escape, it doesn't count unless there are witnesses, and the best witnesses are newspaper reporters.

"Most of my success in Europe," Houdini later wrote, "was due to the fact that I lost no time in stirring up local interest in every town I played. The first thing was to break out of jail." It was especially newsworthy if the jail was a famous one. In Sheffield, England, Houdini made a point of escaping from the cell that had imprisoned Charles Peace—a notorious burglar who had terrorized London. Houdini was stripped, searched, manacled, and then placed in the cell that had been triple-locked. His clothes were placed in a different triple-locked cell. An iron gate leading to the cellblock was also locked. It took Houdini only five minutes to escape, retrieve his clothes, and dress before appearing before the surprised constable. The incident was written up in almost every newspaper. And, of course, his performance later that evening was packed.

"The first thing was to break out of jail."

—Harry Houdini

German officials required that Houdini's act be cleared by the police before he could perform it in a theater. The police didn't welcome any challenge to their authority and they were particularly interested in exposing frauds. When Houdini traveled to Berlin to perform in September of 1900, he first had to prove himself at the police headquarters in front of 300 policemen. He was stripped, his mouth was bandaged shut, and his arms were fastened behind his back with thumbscrews, finger locks, and five different kinds of manacles. He concealed himself by working under a blanket. In about six minutes

This poster on a London street advertised Houdini's appearance at an Orpheum theater.

he emerged and laid the shackles neatly on the table. For his efforts he received a certificate from the police president attesting to the authenticity of his escape.

In Russia, Houdini escaped a Siberian Transport Cell or "Carette." This was the carriage that took exiled prisoners to Siberia and was supposed to be escape-proof. It was described as "a large, somber looking wagon…like a large safe on wheels." One key locked the door and a different key opened it. The key that could release him was located in a prison camp in Siberia, a 20 day journey from Moscow. The "window" in the carriage was a barred slit about 30 inches above the keyhole. Houdini's only stipulation was that

Houdini is about to step into a Siberian Transport Cell in this Russian poster. His escape captured the imagination of the Russian people.

Chief of the Secret Russian Police LEBEDOEFF has HARRY HOUDINI stripped stark naked and searched then locked up in the Siberian Transport Cell or Carette, May 10/1903 in Moscow and in 28 minutes HOUDINI had made his escape to the unspeakable astonishment of the Russian Police.

ПОЛИЦ УПРАВ

HOUDINI in Russia.

the carriage be parked
with the slit against the
wall so that no one
could see him work the
lock. It took him about

POLICE STATE

The government of a police state uses police, especially secret police, to exercise strict or repressive control over the population.

45 minutes, but he escaped by cutting an opening in the floor and repairing it so that no one would notice. The police were focused on him escaping through the door. They figured that he would have needed some kind of extension to reach the lock, and nothing was found on his naked body. They even strip-searched his assistant, Franz Kukol, for such a device but none was found. The police were angry that he escaped, and the story was withheld from the press. Nevertheless, the news spread by word of mouth. Russia was a brutal police state where ordinary people lived in fear. Harry Houdini, who could escape from their most formidable prisons, was more than a hero. He gave them hope and something to cheer for.

Houdini's popularity led to a lot of imitators, and he was extremely protective of his reputation as the first and best self-liberator. He complained, "In England we have 55 Kings of Handcuffs…if you throw a stone in the air it will fall down and hit some one who has a handcuff key in his pocket or a 'handcuff' idea in his head." If imitation is the highest form of flattery, Houdini should have been honored. But he complained that imitators not only copied his tricks and his stage manner, but even tried to use

SLANDER

Slander is the act of making a false or malicious claim that damages a person's reputation.

variations on his name—Hourdene, Whodini, Cutini, Stillini, Nordini, and so on.

Only his brother, Theo, who was also a magician, had Harry's blessing. When Houdini first saw how much work there was in Europe he wired his brother, "Come over, the apples are ripe." When Theo arrived he found that Harry had set him up with equipment, handcuffs, a girl assistant, and had decided on "Hardeen" as his professional name, a name similar to his. Over the years, Houdini and Hardeen used their friendly rivalry to

A police presence made a lock-up appear even more secure. Houdini made friends with police departments around the world.

CIRCUS BUSCH

Houdini

promote both their acts.

In 1902, a German newspaper published an article called "The Unmasking of Houdini." Houdini was accused of attempting to bribe a policeman named Graff into helping him escape from jail, and paying another man to help him with a phony public performance. The accusation may have been a response to the escape he had pulled the previous year in front of the police department, which some officers had found humiliating. An irate Houdini hired a well-known German lawyer to sue both the newspaper and the policeman Graff for slander.

Kaiser Wilhelm II

Life in Germany under Kaiser Wilhelm II was strictly regulated. The Kaiser had been brought up as a military man and was extremely authoritarian. At that time, Germany was developing its iron and steel industry, which required many workers. The Kaiser promoted changes that favored the rich, and the poor workers suffered as a result.

The trial received widespread coverage, only adding to the growing Houdini legend. Harry strongly denied both charges in court, arguing that Graff had tried to deceive him by providing a non-working lock and that he had paid the other man as a thank-you for warning him about the fixed lock.

After many witnesses for both sides succeeded only in confusing the issue, the judge asked Houdini if he could get out of Graff's lock without using tools. Houdini showed the judge in private how he could open the lock by banging it against a metal plate strapped below his knee under his trousers. He won his case, but later complained to a friend, "In order to save my honor I had to show how I did it."

However, the free publicity was probably worth it. He had taken on the police and won. Harry later commented, "…people over here …fear the Police so much, and I am the first man that has ever dared them." Houdini represented more than simply escaping police authority when he escaped from handcuffs and jail cells. He became the idea of escape—the self-liberator—who could free himself from all the things the kept most people captive. At that particular time in history, before World War I erupted in Europe, many people

This ticket allowed admittance to a show where Houdini was the star.

were feeling particularly trapped by political and economic circumstances. Harry Houdini represented freedom. His timing couldn't have been more perfect.

Although times were favorable to Houdini's success, he didn't rely on newspaper articles to promote his show. Posters, flyers, and leaflets were distributed everywhere. One account said that in seven months in England he had used

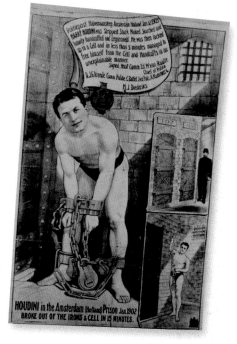

Houdini's naked escape from a jail in Holland is promoted in this poster. Houdini was one of the first truly international superstars.

more than 36 thousand advertising sheets. He ran full-page ads in newspapers, made eye-catching displays for lobbies of important buildings, and in 1903 put together a twelve-page booklet called *America's Sensational Perplexer*. In it he described all the crowds he had drawn and the admission records he had broken. According to Houdini himself, he was "the best advertised man that ever crossed the vaudeville stage in Europe." Not only did Harry work hard, he also worked smart.

chapter 8

Harry and His Family

When Bess Houdini met Harry she had been in her own singing and dancing group. However, if she had hoped for a career of her own, it didn't happen. Her life was now about supporting Harry's ambitions, as his stage assistant and traveling companion. Early in their marriage, they became a true team, working hard to establish a name and to get a big break to earn money. As Harry put it they were "two young people … roaming around trying to make an honest million." Bess gave up a lot to be married to Harry. They lived like nomads, without a home base for many years. Occasionally Bess sulked and refused to go on stage, so Houdini hired other assistants.

For a long time, Bess's mother refused to accept her husband because of his religion. The rift

Bess was only 18 when Harry first met her. He often referred to her as "My large wife." She was barely five feet tall and weighed about 90 pounds.

between them finally ended when Bess became ill, and Harry went to see his mother-in-law with one of his brothers. They refused to leave until Bess's mother agreed to come to the Houdini home to visit Bess. "Thereafter," says Bess, "he was the same as a son to her."

In 1904, the Houdinis left Europe for a two-month summer vacation in America. Harry spent $25,000 to buy a beautiful, elegant townhouse in New York at 278 West 113th Street, near Columbia University and at the edge of Harlem, which was a German neighborhood in those days. He felt that his German-speaking mother would be comfortable in the neighborhood. The house was four stories tall and had 27 rooms. It became the residence of Harry's mother, Cecilia, and his sister, Gladys. Harry and Bess stayed there when they could, which wasn't often. From time to time, it was used by other relatives as well. Harry's brother, Leopold, who became a doctor, set up his office in the house.

Harry and Bess's marriage lasted 32 years. They had a huge party in Hollywood to celebrate their twenty-fifth anniversary.

Harry's devotion to Bess is well documented in thousands of love notes and letters. He called her "Adorable," "Sunshine of my life," and "My Life's Helpmate," signing himself as "the rube who is stuck on you." Bess claimed that every morning she awoke to a note on her pillow. It was a great disappointment to both of them that they had no children. They lavished their affection on their pet dogs and took their pets along on their travels. Harry and Bess were very private about their marriage. His career depended on having trustworthy confederates—people who knew how he did his tricks and could keep them secret. His wife was certainly at the top of that list.

His brother Theo, or "Dash," was also on the list, but for a different reason. Theo had his own career as Houdini's main rival, Hardeen. He did the same handcuff and straitjacket escapes and used all the same secrets. Amazingly, Hardeen had no problem living in his older brother's shadow. Although he was as

Houdini made a point of supporting his brother's career, and officially passed on his "secrets" in his will.

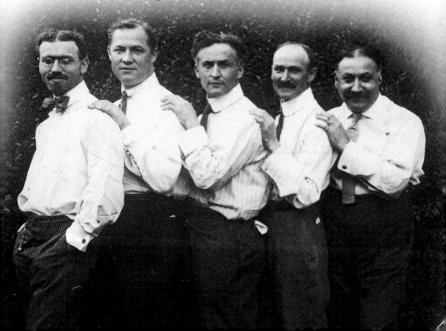

proficient as Harry at performing the same tricks and escapes, he didn't have the personality to connect with an audience the way Harry did and was content to be promoted by his brother as "Houdini's number one rival."

All of the brothers were good friends and liked to spend time together whenever they could. In the fall of 1905, Harry and Theo took a trip back to their old neighborhood in Appleton, Wisconsin, and made a point of having their picture taken in the park where their parents had often sat. The *Appleton Daily Post* ran a story that "the handcuff king still claims Appleton as his home and has advertised the city more than any other person living or dead."

Theo also married and had two sons. At one point,

The Weiss brothers gathered at a family reunion for this portrait. From left to right (youngest to oldest), they are: Leo, Hardeen, Harry, Bill, and Nat.

Harry and Bess spent a year and a half living with Hardeen's family but they eventually moved out. Perhaps it was hard for them to live with nephews who reminded them of the children they didn't have. Of all his family members, Harry Houdini was closest to his mother, Cecilia. He wanted to please her and have her take pleasure in his success. He often brought her to his performances and took her shopping. When they were separated, he wrote often, and he saved

Here, Houdini is shown giving his mother a kiss in Rochester, New York, in 1908.

every one of her letters to him. He had fulfilled his promise to his father to take care of her financially, yet he wanted to do more. During the summer of 1901 he saw a dress in a London shop that had been made for Queen Victoria, who had died before she could wear it. Harry bought it for his mother for $150 (more than $3,000 in today's money), and Bess did the alterations so that it would fit. Then Harry brought his mother to Europe so she could see his act at a sold-out performance in Germany.

But Harry wasn't finished honoring his beloved mother. The next day the Houdinis and Mrs. Weiss took the train to Budapest, the city she had left more than 20 years earlier. Houdini rented a ballroom in the fanciest hotel in Budapest and arranged for a fabulous party. Relatives and friends from his mother's past were invited. She wore Queen Victoria's dress and sat in a gilded chair as she greeted her guests. Houdini later wrote, "How my heart warmed to see various friends and relatives kneel and pay homage to Mother, every inch a Queen. Mother and I were awake all night talking over the affair, and if happiness ever entered my life to its fullest, it was sharing Mother's wonderful enjoyment at playing a queen for a day." Years later Houdini wrote that this was the happiest day of his life.

Queen Victoria

Queen Victoria became the Queen of England in 1837 when she was just 18 years old. She ruled until her death in 1901, becoming the longest reigning monarch in British history. During her reign, Britain became an empire and Victoria herself became an icon and beloved symbol for the British people.

chapter 9

The Scholar and Author

Houdini was constantly searching for ways to improve his act and add to his repertoire of magic tricks. One source of information was magicians of the past, and not just Robert-Houdin. In London, in 1903, Harry met an old man, Henry Evanion, who had a collection of magician's materials—playbills, advertisements, books, and equipment going back almost 200 years. From Evanion, Harry bought many of the items that became the core of his own library and collection of magic memorabilia, a collection that eventually filled the fourth floor of his New York home.

He was also interested in speaking to retired magicians.

That same year, in Germany, Houdini made several attempts to meet with 87-year-old Wiljaba Frikell. Frikell was considered the first "modern" magician (although some claim this title for Robert-Houdin). He had appeared on stage

Harry's Collection

Houdini's collection of magic literature, playbills, engravings, and photographs filled the fourth floor rooms of his home in New York. He hired an Englishman, Alfred Becks, to organize his collection. Becks had been in charge of the theater library at Harvard University. It took him almost two years of living and working in Houdini's house to make order out of the chaos.

in everyday clothes instead of a flowing wizard gown, and used ordinary objects in his act. Finally, a meeting was set. The old man prepared for Houdini's visit at his home by bringing out his research materials, polishing his medals, and displaying photographs. However, two hours before the scheduled visit, Frikell died of a heart attack. Mrs. Frikell met Houdini at the door. Later Houdini recalled, "There we stood together, the woman who had loved the dear old wizard for years and the young magician who had been so willing to love him had he been allowed to know him." Frikell and Evanion were father figures to Houdini, who missed his own father terribly. Mrs. Frikell gave Houdini her husband's wand, but many of his secrets, which Harry yearned to know, died with the old man.

When Houdini returned to the United States in 1905 he began to fulfill another of his ambitions: to become a writer. Scholarship—

Harry poses with older magician Ira Davenport, who inspired him to become an escape artist.

Houdini worked long hours in this over-crowded study in New York.

studying and writing—are embedded in Jewish culture, and perhaps Harry wanted to do something that would have made his father proud. Harry was aware that his formal education was lacking, but, if anything, that shortcoming spurred him on to become self-educated. He taught himself to type (at 80 words a minute, he bragged) and took his typewriter with him everywhere. He had no trouble getting words onto paper, although spelling and grammatical errors found their way into everything he wrote. His first book, *The Right Way to Do Wrong,* was published in 1906. It explained the various ways burglars break and enter. Houdini was interested in all kinds of trickery, both legal and criminal, in order to understand how to mystify people. He was committed to exposing frauds and criminals so that he himself could not be considered at odds with the law. Although *The Right Way to Do Wrong* revealed the methods of con men and swindlers as an anti-crime book, it was banned in Germany. German authorities were afraid that criminals would use it as a training manual. In fact, criminals all over the world bought it to take it out of circulation because they did not want their methods to become public knowledge.

That year Houdini also started *Conjurers' Monthly* magazine. The magazine concentrated on the history of magic and included articles demolishing his imitators and enemies. He was obsessed with constantly proving that he was the best and setting himself apart from the people copying or stealing his most effective tricks. In fact, so many people were doing handcuff escapes that Dr. A. M. Wilson, publisher of *The Sphinx* (the only magazine to rival *Conjurer's Monthly*), said that these acts were so common they would soon be seen only in dime museums. Houdini took offense that Wilson was implying that his act was cheap. Although he was a major star on the vaudeville circuit, he was still doing many of the tricks he had performed in his dime museum days. This began a feud between Houdini and Wilson that spilled over into the Society of American Magicians (SAM), a fraternity or fellowship of professionals

The first issue of *Conjurers' Monthly* featured articles on "Handcuff Secrets," "Reading and Rubbish," and intenational news.

in the field. Harry wanted the organization to adopt his magazine as its official journal. In 1908, when they refused, he resigned from SAM and announced it in his next issue (although he would later rejoin and be elected president). If Harry Houdini was seeking recognition from other magicians he was going about it in the wrong way.

Throughout his career, Houdini was extremely competitive—he needed to be considered top in his field. It is in the nature of show business for performers to call themselves "the greatest." Houdini began his shows by telling his audience just how great he was. Some people found this tiresome, but others felt that boastfulness was a part of the personality required for a star of Houdini's stature. Although Houdini knew many magicians socially, he would often put them down when he spoke about them privately. Another way of proving his superiority was to reveal how others did their tricks.

Houdini poses with his book: *The Unmasking of Robert-Houdin,* which he hoped would live on as a history of magic.

This was in violation of a code among magicians and went against a professed purpose of SAM. Houdini was not above calling a rival a fraud in public. If there was an uproar and it made the papers, so much the better. For Houdini there was no such thing as bad publicity. The only magicians he seemed to truly care about were dead ones. Houdini would visit their graves and make sure their grave sites were tended to. In his mind, if they were not performing they could not be rivals.

SAM

The Society of American Magicians was founded in New York on May 10, 1902. Its purpose was to promote magic as an art form and encourage harmony among magicians. It also took a stand against exposing the secrets of magicians—how tricks are achieved. Four years later, SAM made Houdini an honorary member, and he appeared at local chapters on behalf on the organization. He was elected president in 1917 and kept that office for the rest of his life.

It may well be that Houdini's anger and frustration with his fellow magicians influenced his book *The Unmasking of Robert-Houdin*, which was published in 1908. The hero who had inspired him as a boy to become a magician, and whose name he used for himself, became for Houdini "a mere pretender, a man who waxed great on the brainwork of others." He claimed that Robert-Houdin did not invent most of the effects he used in his performances and that he didn't give proper credit to the originators (including Frikell).

In Houdini's opinion, Robert-Houdin was not skilled in sleight of hand, and his book, *Memoirs,* was more fiction than fact. He accused Robert-Houdin of using a Paris journalist as a ghostwriter. In attacking Houdin's book, Houdini created an uproar. The French in particular were outraged that Houdini called the man they considered the father of modern magic a "prince of pilferers." But Houdini himself had ambitions for this book, which he felt

This poster advertises the act of Harry Kellar, Houdini's most famous predecessor. Kellar was considered the "dean" of American magicians.

embodied a history of magic. In his own opinion, "*Robert-Houdin Unmasked*…will live long after we are all dead, will stand as a monument of years of diligent research and endeavor, and will bring me back to the minds of the public when I am long forgotten as a public performer." The immodest Houdini felt that his writings would be yet another form of immortality.

Despite Houdini's desire to place himself above his competitors, there were a few magicians that Houdini truly respected and considered giants in the field. Harry Kellar

(1849–1922) was Houdini's true professional "father." Kellar was the first American magician to become an international star. He had invented a knot that was easy to escape and taught it to Houdini. His trademark trick was making a girl appear to float in midair.

Howard Thurston (1869–1936) became Kellar's official heir when he received the older magician's wand at a retirement ceremony. He was known as the "King of Cards" and made playing cards appear to float in the air from his outstretched fingers. He was the only one of Houdini's contemporaries to have a huge international career and his own movie studio. Houdini had a guarded but friendly relationship with him.

T. Nelson Downs (1867–1838) was also known as the "King of Koins." He was a master of coin manipulation, making coins appear and disappear. He wrote two "how-to" books that were the first of their kind to explain tricks. He and Houdini spent hours discussing the fine points of their profession and Houdini never spoke ill of him.

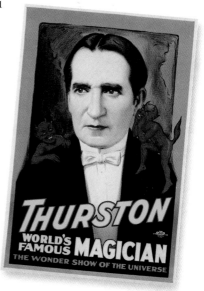

Howard Thurston became Houdini's most famous rival. He was Kellar's official successor and paid him a royalty for the use of some of his secrets.

10

Taking Risks

When Houdini returned to the United States in 1905, he made a deliberate shift from being a magician who does some escapes to being a true escape artist. He also added a new kind of publicity stunt—jumping off bridges while handcuffed and chained. Escape from the irons required Houdini's usual trickery, but jumping off a bridge into cold water required additional training. Houdini was

Houdini is shackled and ready to jump. Crowds line the bridge while Bess stands behind him in an outstanding hat.

already a diligent and disciplined athlete. He had learned to swim as a boy in the turbulent

"Only feel good after one of these baths."

–Harry Houdini

currents of the East River off Manhattan. He had trained himself at age 18 to hold his breath for a record 3 minutes, 45 seconds. Now, upon his return to New York, he had Bess help him practice holding his breath underwater. He had lost some of his lung capacity as he had grown older. Bess timed him with a stopwatch and he managed to get back to three minutes, which gave him plenty of time to get out of his manacles. To help strengthen his lungs he began running daily.

Even if he could hold his breath, it was a challenge just to function with the shock of cold water on his body. This, too, required training. Every morning at 7:00 (after giving two performances the evening before) Harry submerged himself in a cold bath. Using ice, he would chill the bath water to 50 degrees Farenheit (10 degrees Celcius) and even lower, until a doctor stopped him. He got used to being cold and wrote in his diary, "Only feel good after one of these baths."

The jump off the Weighlock Bridge in Rochester, New York, on May 6, 1907, is preserved on film. It is typical of the many promotional bridge jumps that Houdini used to advertise his appearance at a local theater. Although the "naked jail cell escape" usually received widespread newspaper coverage and he still did it in every major city, the bridge jumps drew an actual crowd. The Weighlock

Bridge spanned the Erie Canal and the water must have been pretty cold on that day in early May. The event was scheduled for 12:30 in the afternoon, but a crowd estimated at 10,000 began gathering two hours earlier. Houdini arrived with his assistant, Franz Kukol, dressed in his formal attire. He stripped down to his long white undershorts and allowed the local police to put two sets of handcuffs on him. Climbing to a beam on top of the bridge, he held up his manacled hands and called, "Good-bye" to the crowd. Then he plunged feet first into the cold, black water. The film showed one pair of cuffs fly off during the trip down. Within 15 seconds, Houdini appeared

Houdini is jumping into the Charles River in Boston. So many boats were around to watch that they created a even more dangers for him.

at the surface with only one pair of the handcuffs dangling from a wrist. He disappeared under the water briefly to retrieve the other cuffs and when he resurfaced he waved both pairs of unlocked handcuffs to the cheering crowd as he swam to shore.

Later that year Houdini jumped into the Mississippi River in New Orleans. This time he was handcuffed behind his back with his elbows pulled together with chains. Houdini actually liked having heavy chains on him because they helped him sink out of sight from the crowd while he freed himself. He did not want the crowd to see how easily he unlocked the cuffs. The currents caught him by surprise, however. "That's an awful river…And the further down I went the colder and darker it became."

If he felt a jump wasn't dangerous enough, Houdini was not above embellishing a story. He claimed that when he jumped off the Belle Island Bridge into the Detroit River, a hole in the ice had to be made for him to enter the water. When he landed in the river, he said that the current pulled him under the ice and he had to swim in ever-widening circles to find the opening, breathing by putting his nose in the tiny space between the water and the ice. The truth is that he did make a jump off the Belle Island Bridge on November 27, 1906, when the temperature was forty-five degrees—very cold, but nowhere near the temperature needed for ice to form. However, his story became a part of the Houdini myth and was repeated after his death by his wife for one of his biographies.

Houdini imagined all kinds of seemingly impossible and dangerous escapes. Handcuffs alone were not enough. He escaped after being shackled and then sealed in a large wooden case that was lowered into a body of water. He escaped after being strapped to a mattress with leather restraints around his ankles, thighs, wrists, and neck. He escaped after being rolled in sheets that were soaked in hot water to make them shrink. No matter how impossible the situations seemed, Houdini escaped them all.

What was the secret to his miraculous escapes? Houdini claimed:

> "My chief task has been to conquer fear. When I am stripped and manacled, nailed securely within a weighted packing case and thrown into the sea…it is necessary to preserve absolute serenity of spirit. I have to work with great delicacy and lightning speed. If I grow panicky I am lost. And if something goes wrong, if there is some little accident or mishap, some

A French biplane, the Voisin was a flimsy affair. It was little more than a box kite with a motor.

slight miscalculation, I am lost unless all my faculties are working on high, free from mental tension or strain. The public sees only the thrill of the accomplished trick; they have no conception of the tortuous preliminary self-training that was necessary to conquer fear. "My second secret has been, by equally vigorous self-training, to enable me to do remarkable things with my body, to make not one muscle or a group of muscles, but every muscle, a responsive worker, quick and sure for its part, to make my fingers super-fingers in dexterity, and to train my toes to do the work of fingers."

If Houdini was a master at jumping down, he was also fascinated with fighting gravity—flying. The Wright brothers had made their first flight in 1903 and had given their first public exhibition in Europe in 1908. In 1909, Houdini saw his first airplane, a French Voisin, and arranged to buy it for about $5,000. It was a flimsy biplane, made of wood and

Birth of Flight

The first powered flight of a heavier-than-air plane took place on December 17, 1903, at Kitty Hawk, North Carolina, in a plane designed and built by Wilbur and Orville Wright. Orville was the pilot of the "Flyer," which was made of wood beams covered with muslin, and was powered by a four-cylinder engine. Without a pilot, it weighed 605 pounds (274 kg). The first flight lasted 12 seconds, went about nine feet up, and traveled a distance of 120 feet (37 meters)—less than half a football field.

canvas, and held together with wire. The exposed aviator had to wear a cap and goggles to keep hair and wind out of his eyes. Harry had "Houdini" painted on the side panels and tail, and hired a French mechanic, Antonio Brassac, to teach him to fly. Flying was a risky business at best. At the time, the speed record in an airplane was 47 miles per hour (76 km/h). At that rate it was hard to get off the ground, harder to stay in the air, and it was very easy to crash.

A few weeks after his first flying lessons, Harry was invited to perform in Melbourne, Australia. Although Houdini accepted travel as a necessary part of his career, Australia was particularly far away and represented an extra long journey by ship. Harry suffered from seasickness on every sea voyage, and the two-month round-trip journey was particularly unappealing. But the theater manager in Melbourne, Australia, promised to pay him extra for his travel time. The other inducement was the invitation of the Aerial League of New South Wales to bring along his biplane and be the first to fly in Australia. The publicity such a flight would generate for both the Aerial League and Houdini was irresistible. So Harry, Bess, Franz Kukol, and Antonio Brassac set sail for the land down under. In the

> *"Freedom and exhilaration, that's what it is."*
>
> –Harry Houdini

ship's hold, packed in crates, was the Voison plane along with a set of extra parts.

Houdini sits in the cockpit of his Voisin. The plane cost him $5,000 and came with a set of plans and extra parts so it could be repaired after the likely event of a crash.

Harry's first task upon arriving in Adelaide, Australia, on February 6, was to gain back the 28 pounds he had lost during the voyage. Then he and his group traveled 400 miles south by train to Melbourne, where he was to perform his magic act. The airfield from which he would fly the Voisin was at Diggers Rest, a flat area cleared of stones and other obstacles about 20 miles north of the city. It took several weeks to reassemble the Voisin and begin testing the aircraft in preparation for his attempt to make the first successful flight in Australia. Houdini was in a hurry because he had some competition. Another pioneer aviator, Ralph Banks, was also in the running at Diggers Rest with a biplane designed by the Wright brothers. However, Banks crashed his plane in an attempt on March 1, taking him out of the contest. In Sydney, 500 miles to the north, an automobile racer, Fred Custance, was also attempting to be the first Australian aviator with a monoplane, or a plane with one wing. On March 17, Custance made three one-mile circles in five and a half minutes. However, he only got 12 feet off the ground, and there were no officials present to witness the flight. According to the rules set up by an international aviation organization, it didn't count.

At Diggers Rest, Houdini and his team had been waiting for clear, windless weather. On March 18, it was finally calm enough for Houdini to make his attempt. On the third try he succeeded. Here is an account of the event from the *Argus*, a Melbourne newspaper:

Even in the air, Houdini wanted everyone to know he was there. The press was invited to witness his historic attempts to be the first to fly in Australia.

"The third flight lasted 3 1/2 min. and was unmarred by any fault. Houdini swept boldly away from the flying field, confident of his control of the plane, and passing over rocky rises and stone fences, described a great circle, which was, at the lowest estimate, well over two miles. The descent was faultless, and the plane came to rest within 20 ft. of the starting point, where the little knot of witnesses were standing."

Houdini was a natural. When asked how he felt about flying Houdini said, "The funny thing was that as soon as I was aloft, all the tension and strain left me....Freedom and exhilaration, that's what it is."

Houdini flew again at Diggers Rest on March 21, staying aloft for seven and a half minutes and covering a distance of six miles. The Australian Aerial League awarded him a trophy as the first successful aviator in their country. To this day, Houdini is given credit for his pioneering aviation work in Australia. After packing up the Voisin to leave Australia, Houdini never flew again.

chapter 11

Houdini's Creativity

In 1910 the Houdinis returned to the United States from Australia for an extended tour. They did not travel lightly and they did not travel alone. The members of Harry's entourage were all sworn to secrecy. In addition to his usual group, Houdini had added a British master mechanic and cabinet maker who could build anything Houdini required, plus two other assistants. When traveling, the team required two railroad cars: one for people and the other for props, equipment, books, and tools. Houdini was frequently short-tempered with his staff and would often fire one or more of them. However, they learned that he didn't ever mean it, and the incident was usually forgotten the next day. Houdini was the inventor and creative force behind all

Houdini was shackled and locked in this crate before being lowered into the East River in New York.

of his tricks. He was an innovative, outside-the-box thinker in all of his endeavors. With all the handcuff imitators, Houdini decided he would have to expand his escape act to include more than just unshackling himself from handcuffs. He invented a new, spectacular underwater box escape, in which he would be manacled before being sealed in a wooden box and lowered into a body of water.

Houdini makes his triumphant escape from the submerged crate.

His first performance was on July 7, 1912, off a pier on the East River in New York. The escape was arranged to promote his opening at Hammerstein's Roof Garden, where he was to be paid his highest salary yet—$1,000.00 per week (nearly $20,000 in today's money). The box was made of sturdy planks weighted with iron and passed the closest inspection. A huge crowd had gathered for the spectacle. At the last moment, just before Houdini was to step into the box, the police showed up and stopped him. It was against the law to jump into the East River. By coincidence (or perhaps an arrangement) there was a tugboat nearby. Houdini, his staff, the press, and his packing case went on board, out of the reach of the police. Houdini was manacled, nailed into the box, and lowered into the swirling waters. It took 57 seconds for him to surface, to the cheers of the fans, press, and police (who had stayed to watch). The packing case was hauled up and opened to reveal all the shackles and leg irons inside. The trick was repeated at his evening show, which featured a large pool of water on stage. At the end of the week, Harry requested his payment in gold coins. He took them to his mother and showered her with the money—fulfilling yet again his father's request that he take care of her financially.

How did he escape? One side panel of the packing case was fastened with special screws whose very short length could not be detected by the inspectors but could be quickly removed by Houdini. After Houdini was nailed into the case, his assistant listened for a short rap that was the signal that Houdini was out of the shackles. The box was not lowered until Houdini was free. Once underwater Houdini could remove the board, get out of the box, and replace the board before surfacing. His confederates found a moment to secretly replace the screws so that the box could pass inspection again.

Houdini was always being challenged to escape unusual devices designed to imprison and torture people. As an expert on many methods of trapping and holding humans, he invented his own version of an underwater escape that he called "The Chinese Water Torture Cell." After three years working on it, Houdini said, "I believe it is the climax of all my studies and labors. Never will I be able to construct anything that will be more dangerous or difficult for me to do." It certainly appeared difficult. The "cell" was a strong mahogany box, about as tall and as wide as Houdini himself. The watertight front panel was made of ½ inch–thick glass so observers could look inside. During a performance, Houdini lay on the stage while stocks were fastened around his ankles. Then he was hoisted up feet first until he was suspended above the cell, now filled with water. At his signal, he was lowered head first into the tank, splashing water onto the stage. The audience was able to see him holding his breath and watch his hair swirling around him in the water. Houdini's assistants stood

Houdini is about to be lowered, upside down, into his famous Water Torture Cell. He called this trick his "upside down," and it became one of his signature stunts.

97

by with an ax to break the glass and save him if necessary. Again, the audience had been reminded with the usual drama that life without air was only possible for a very short time.

The ghost house was closed around the seemingly doomed magician. Then, in less than two minutes, Houdini reappeared, drenched and triumphant, to the thunderous applause of the audience. The trick was so dangerous to perform (even if the escape itself was not difficult) that Houdini felt it would not be as widely copied as the milk-can escape he had introduced in 1908. Only a few people today know the secret of how he did it.

Houdini's preoccupation with escaping from underwater traps prompted him to invent a diver's suit for deep sea dives. He had noticed that the diving suits that were currently in use were difficult to get into and out of. Houdini's invention was designed to "permit the diver, in case of any danger…to quickly divest himself of the suit while being submerged and to safely escape and reach the surface." The suit was designed to permit the diver to get in and out without help

DETAIL

Houdini included this sketch when applying for a patent for his fast-escape diving suit. It could be put on without assistance and could be shed in as little as 45 seconds.

and prevent him from being crushed by the water if the air supply suddenly was cut off. Houdini received a patent for his invention on March 1, 1921.

As he got older, Houdini wanted to add some magic illusions to his act that didn't require so much from his body. One illusion was called "Walking Through a Brick Wall." Workmen constructed a brick wall on stage. It was built on a steel beam on wheels, raising it

One of the first truly international stars, Houdini is the "Master of Mystery" in this French poster.

two inches off the ground. The end of the wall faced the audience so that they could see both sides, and a screen that was shorter than the wall but taller than Houdini was placed around it. Houdini was hidden, but made his presence known by waving his hand above the screen and crying, "Here I am!" The screen was immediately folded back to show the side of the wall Houdini had indicated with the hand wave. Houdini was not there. Then the screen concealing the opposite side of the wall was removed and there was the magician, smiling and waving.

There was a carpet under the wall. Houdini assured the crowd that the carpet made certain he couldn't use a trap door and the two-inch elevation of the steel beam was much too narrow to allow him under the wall. The screens would not conceal him going over or around the wall. But in fact, the trick did depend on a trap door under the wall. When the trap door was open, the carpet sagged just enough for Houdini to squeeze under the beam. It was closed as soon as he passed through so no one could detect it.

Houdini's other major illusion was Jenny, his vanishing elephant, introduced in 1918. Jenny was, according to Houdini, "the biggest vanish the world has ever seen." After giving Houdini a kiss with her trunk and receiving a cube

Jenny was the daughter of "Jumbo," the star of P. T. Barnum's circus. Jenny weighed in between 2 and 5 tons—Houdini was deliberately vague about her actual size.

of sugar from him in return, Jenny walked into a super-sized ghost house. Two seconds later, Houdini opened the ghost house and the elephant had disappeared. "Even the elephant doesn't know how it's done," Houdini quipped. The secret: the elephant walked into another cabinet immediately behind the one the audience saw. The illusion was pulled off too quickly to give anyone time to

Houdini liked to do his own stunts whenever possible. Here he lowers himself onto the wing of a plane.

think about it. Houdini had bought both of these spectacular illusions from the magicians who had invented them. Buying and selling tricks was a common practice among professional magicians. Hardeen did most of the same tricks Houdini performed with his brother's blessing. But it was up to each magician to add his own interpretation, and Houdini's showmanship elevated each stunt to a whole new level.

In 1918 show business was starting to change. Movies had started to catch on. Stars of vaudeville were in demand by early film makers, and Houdini could not resist contributing to the new medium. His first movie, *Master Mystery*, was

Movies

The first film to depict a story was produced by Thomas Edison (1847–1931) and his assistant William Kennedy (1860–1935). It was called *The Great Train Robbery*, consisted of 14 scenes, and was 10 minutes long. It played in Philadelphia, Pennsylvania, in a theater called a "nickelodeon" because the price of admission was five cents.

a serial of fifteen episodes with a complicated plot. Each episode showed him escaping some life-threatening danger using his remarkable techniques. In one, he picked a lock using an umbrella rib and a piece of string. In another, he opened a door while chained to a wall using his toes to turn the key.

Houdini planned the plots of each episode so that it highlighted his skills and daring. In *The Grim Game,* the script called for him to jump from the wing of one plane onto the wing of another in midair. However, when the scene was shot, the two planes tangled briefly before they separated and crashed, all of which was filmed, and the scene ended up in the movie. Fortunately, no one was killed in the accident, and Houdini was never in danger because a stunt double was used. (Athough he had planned to do all his own stunt work, he had injured

In Houdini's last movie, he played a man from another age who comes to life after being frozen in ice.

HOUDINI PICTURE CORPORATION

presents

HOUDINI

in

"THE MAN FROM BEYOND"

his arm during a previous shot and was unable to perform.) However, Houdini didn't want people to know about the stunt double. Defying death was part of his image.

Houdini was not a great success as a film star. All together he made five movies, and none of them were box office successes. His live performances were exciting partly because something could go wrong at any moment. People knew that stunts on film could be faked. However, appearing in the movies did serve one purpose—it made him even more famous. Houdini never regarded his foray into the movies a failure. Like his flirtation with aviation, he had his fling with the movies and moved on.

Houdini escapes the savages in his movie *Terror Island*. Some people felt that his acting was stiff, particularly when he had to do love scenes.

chapter 12

Defying Death

O ne of the most traumatic events in Harry Houdini's life was the death of his mother on July 17, 1913. Houdini received the cable from his brother Theo after a performance in Copenhagen. He and Bess had just arrived in Europe, and his mother had seen them off on the boat only 11 days before. Bess had recorded their last good-bye in her journal:

Houdini commissioned this impressive monument at his mother's grave site.

"Persons at the pier beheld a curious sight. They saw Houdini clinging to a little old woman in black silk, embracing and kissing her, saying good-bye and going up the gangplank, only to return to embrace her again…she had to order him to go. Houdini, turning to the bystanders, said, 'Look, my mother drives me away from her.' 'No, No,' protested his mother, 'but you must leave now. Go quickly, and come back safe to me.'" He was the last person up the gangplank.

Houdini was so shocked at the news of his mother's death that he fainted. When he came to, weeping, he canceled the rest of

Houdini hangs upside-down over Broadway, confined in a straightjacket.

his tour and he and Bess took the next boat home. It is Jewish custom to bury the dead within 48 hours, but Harry wired his brother to delay the funeral so he could view her body one last time. Just before he left, Cecilia had asked her son to bring her back some woolen bedroom slippers. Harry brought them with him, and they were placed in her coffin.

Harry was grief stricken. He spent the month of August visiting his mother's grave in Queens, New York, every day.

A publicity poster boasts of Houdini's victory over Rahman Bey.

Later, Houdini wrote, "I who have laughed at the terrors of death, who have smilingly leaped from high bridges, received a shock from which I do not think recovery is possible." He did not work for several months, and when he returned to his tour of Europe, his heart was not in it. But his publicity stunts were becoming more risky—jumping from bridges, being thrown into water in packing cases, and hanging upside-down outside buildings as he wriggled out of a straitjacket. He tried being manacled and buried alive. But earth is not water. He started with shallow "graves" one or two feet deep, which were not a problem. Four- and five-foot graves were more difficult. But Houdini wanted to escape a real grave that was six feet deep. Only with an enormous struggle did he get himself out. He himself admitted later that he had nearly killed himself. He never again tried this skirmish with death.

It was important to Houdini's image that he appear to be an invincible hero. However, the nature of his work caused wear and tear on his body, and he was nearing 40. He knew how important his health was and he never smoked or drank liquor, but he did get injured. On more than one occasion, an escape caused bruising and swelling of his hands and arms. Years of jerking out of a straitjacket caused a cyst on his buttocks that required minor surgery. He had injured his kidney escaping from a large strapped bag in 1911. An aching kidney became a lasting reminder of his body's vulnerability and a source of concern for the rest of his life. Being hauled upside down to escape a straitjacket or go into the "Chinese Water Torture Cell" strained his ankles. Every so often, Houdini would complain about being worn out and announce that he would soon be retiring from show business. However, if he did retire, it was never

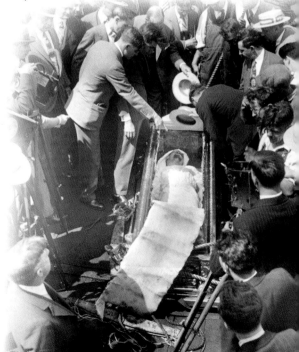

Rahman Bey is pulled from his casket in the Hudson River.

for long. He could stand a lot of pain and he wanted the show to go on.

The death of his mother often made Houdini think about his own death. Over the years, a number of his own escapes were out of coffins. One of his last challenges in the summer of 1926 was to beat Rahman Bey, an Egyptian fakir, or religious mystic, at his own game. Bey had boasted that he could stay submerged in the Hudson River in New York in a bronze casket for an hour. At the time, he was currently appearing on Broadway, where he lay in a casket that was then buried in sand. He claimed that he put himself into a trance where his need for air was greatly reduced. But Houdini knew the trick. A friend of Houdini's saw a crack at the head of the coffin large enough for a breathing straw. Houdini would not let Bey go on unchallenged.

When Bey's first test took place, he rang an emergency bell four minutes after he had been sealed inside the casket, before it was lowered into the water. It took workmen 15 minutes to chisel him out, so he avoided embarrassment by claiming that he had gone without air for 20 minutes. Houdini thought that he was a fraud and called him so in public. Bey responded by staying in a sealed zinc casket for a total of 49 minutes, 24 minutes of it underwater in a swimming pool. Houdini had a coffin made that contained about 34 cubic inches of air—enough air to last a person three or four minutes. It had a glass top so that a doctor could keep an eye on Houdini in case his life appeared to be in danger. It was submerged in a pool and Houdini stayed in it for an hour and 31 minutes. There was no trick to this event. Houdini simply remained calm, made no unnecessary movements, and breathed shallowly. When he emerged from the coffin his pulse was very fast, he was dripping with perspiration, and he was deathly white. It took him a day or so to recover. Houdini felt that what he learned from this experience would be of value for miners and submariners and others who may be trapped with a limited amount of air.

Houdini prepares to answer Rahman Bey's challenge and stay submerged in a casket for over an hour and a half.

chapter 13

The Dead Don't Talk

Houdini originally got the idea to become an escape artist from the Davenport Brothers when he was still "Dime Museum Harry." Ira and William Davenport were medium magicians. Medium magicians explained their illusions as being caused by supernatural forces. One of the Davenports' most famous feats was to have themselves tied up on benches in a cabinet so that they couldn't move. Musical instruments were then placed on a shelf in the cabinet and the doors were closed. Instantly, all the instruments began playing at once. When the doors were thrown open the brothers were still tied in place and the instruments were still on the shelf. Their manager claimed that their powers came from spirits, or the souls of dead people, who could be reached by the brothers who were mediums to the departed,

Houdini produced a lecture and show disproving spirit mediums.

MEDIUM

A medium claims to be able to convey messages between living people and the spirits of the dead.

and that through them the dead could communicate with the living.

People who believed that spirits could talk to the living were called "spiritualists." The effects of the Davenport brothers were simple tricks. They never actually claimed to be spiritualists, but they let people believe what they wanted to believe. They had techniques for escaping the ropes that bound them—the same methods that Harry learned and used to elevate escapism itself to a form of entertainment.

In 1897, a young Houdini had given a public performance of a séance—a session where the medium produces supernatural effects including messages from the dead. But it left him with a bad feeling. He didn't like fooling people by exploiting their loss of a loved one. He thought it was okay to trick people, lie, and fabricate stories for the purpose of

A "Spirit Photograph" shows Houdini with the long-dead Abraham Lincoln. In the early days of photography, not many understood how to produce an image like this.

entertainment, but it was wrong to take people's money, play on their emotions, and manipulate them into thinking he could truly connect them to a dead person.

However, these beliefs didn't stop other people from becoming mediums, holding séances, and advertising phony psychic abilities. Spiritualism became a popular phenomenon, especially after World War I when so many people had lost loved ones in the war and wanted to speak to them one last time. But spiritualism became more than just a means of communicating with the dead—it became a kind of religion. Mediums presented evidence of the spirit world, called "spiritualistic manifestations." During a séance, knocks were heard, bells rang, objects flew through the air, tables levitated, and screens fell over. Sometimes the medium would produce a "spirit hand" made of wax, or a "spirit photo" which showed ghostlike images next to the image of a real person. Some mediums produced "ectoplasm," a kind of gooey material that flowed from the ear, mouth, or nose; could take different shapes, including that of a face; and was explained as evidence of life after death. During séances, the medium was "controlled." This meant that he or she held hands with the neighbor on each side and had each foot pressed

World War I Losses

World War I deaths among the allied powers, including the United States and Britain, totaled 5.5 million soldiers and 6.5 million civilians. It was, at that time, the bloodiest war the world had ever seen.

against a neighbor's foot, so that any motion the medium might make to produce the "supernatural" effects could be detected. Since most people didn't have any idea how these events could be made to happen by ordinary means, they truly believed that they were in the presence of a medium to the spirit world. We know today that spiritualistic manifestations were simply tricks well known to professional magicians.

A Famous Friend

Sir Arthur Conan Doyle (1859–1930) was a physician and politician as well as a writer. He was knighted for his service as a doctor in the Boer War in South Africa in 1900. He and Houdini shared many interests that allowed them to be friends until their disagreement about spiritualism led to a falling out.

One of the main champions of spiritualism was Sir Arthur Conan Doyle, the famous British author of the popular Sherlock Holmes mysteries. He became famous for his lectures on spiritualism. His talks were given in a straightforward, matter-of-fact manner. He showed a spirit photo of himself and his dead son and another of an Armistice Day crowd in London with a sky full of the heads of dead soldiers from the War. Houdini had met Doyle in 1920 after sending him a copy of his book *The Unmasking of Robert-Houdin.*

113

Houdini, who was always conscious of his lack of a formal education, appreciated it when well-educated

ARMISTICE DAY

Armistice Day was an annual celebration of the end of World War I on November 11, 1918. It was incorporated into the observance of Veterans Day in 1954.

people treated him as an equal. A friendship developed that included their wives and involved visiting each other's homes on both sides of the Atlantic. Doyle objected to a sentence in Houdini's book that suggested that the Davenport Brothers' work was due to trickery rather than spiritualistic manifestations. At first, Houdini did not openly disagree with Doyle. He was enjoying the friendship—and perhaps he wished that spiritualism was not the hoax he believed it was. Wouldn't it be wonderful if his beloved mother could contact him from beyond the grave? On the other hand, Houdini was determined to expose mediums as frauds who used the tricks of a magician to produce their effects. Doyle was a highly visible spokesman for spiritualism with

Spirits were supposed to write directly on a slate during a séance. Here, Houdini reveals how tablets are switched to fool believers.

a lot of followers. If Houdini could prove him wrong, it would enhance his own reputation—although it might cost him a friendship.

In the spring of 1922, when they were in America for a lecture tour, the Doyles visited the Houdinis. Lady Doyle, Sir Doyle's wife, who claimed to be a medium herself, agreed to give a private séance for Harry so that he could contact his mother. Lady Doyle would do "automatic writing," which means that the words she wrote would be a kind of dictation from the spirit world. At the séance Harry closed his eyes and tried to get into the mood. A pad and pencil were placed before Lady Doyle. She

Sir Arthur Conan Doyle's wife, Jean, conducted the séance for Harry on his mother's birthday. That fact never came up during the séance, adding to Harry's skepticism.

began striking the table, which meant that a spirit was present. Was it the spirit of Cecelia Weiss? Again three knocks signaled "yes." Houdini later wrote that he was "waiting for a sign or vibrations, feeling for the presence of my dearly beloved Mother." Lady Doyle began writing. She began by making a cross at the top of the page. During the séance she filled fifteen sheets of paper with writing that was supposed to be Cecelia Weiss speaking to her son. Houdini didn't say anything to her after the séance, but he was more convinced than ever that spiritualism was a fraud. His Jewish mother would never put a cross on the top of a page, she didn't speak English, the language of the automatic writing, and none of the familiar subjects he had always discussed with his mother showed up. Nevertheless, Harry concealed his misgivings about the séance from the Doyles. He didn't want to stir up trouble with his friends. But he later became determined to expose mediums publicly as frauds.

In order to uncover the truth, Houdini attended many séances dressed in disguise as a "Mr. White." Sometimes he would jump up and expose tricks on the spot, revealing his true identity. Other times he made notes and typed them up later. He first went public with his findings in a newspaper article in 1922 where he stated that he had "never seen or heard anything that could convince me that there is a possibility of communication with the loved ones who have gone beyond." This ruffled the feathers of the proponents of spiritualism, including Sir Arthur Conan

Doyle, who was hurt that his friend hadn't believed in Lady Doyle's psychic abilities.

LEGERDEMAIN

Legerdemain is a display of skill or cleverness, especially for deceitful purposes.

The controversy between Houdini and the spiritualists came to a head in 1924. *Scientific American* was a distinguished and highly respected monthly magazine founded in 1845. It published articles on a variety of subjects, including research into the human mind. In January 1924 it announced a contest offering $2,500 to anyone who could scientifically prove that their spiritualistic manifestations were real. A five-member committee would choose the winner. Houdini was a member of the committee because, as he put it, "It takes a flimflammer to catch a flimflammer."

He also said, "I am prepared to reproduce any signal or bit of legerdemain they [mediums] use no matter how unearthly it may seem to the untrained observer." One medium who came forward early was quickly

Houdini shows how a medium could slip a foot out of a shoe to ring a bell while the man sitting opposite tries to feel movement with his own foot.

117

exposed by Houdini, scaring off other potential candidates for several months.

Mina Crandon was the beautiful young wife of a prominent Boston surgeon, Dr. L. G. Crandon. She claimed to have discovered her psychic gifts after her marriage, and gave private séances in the Crandon home without charging a fee. She did not want publicity, and did not use her real name as a psychic. Instead, she called herself "Margery." Margery's séances were held in the dark, and people held hands in a circle. Margery would go into a trance and speak in several languages. There were raps, a levitating table top, and flickering lights, accompanied by the presence of a spirit named "Walter," Margery's dead brother. Walter was foul-mouthed and rowdy when he spoke, so different from his refined, ladylike sister that he came across as a separate person in spite of the fact that the voice came from Margery. He made the séances so entertaining that Margery became somewhat famous in Europe as well as in the Boston area. She became the prime contender for the *Scientific American* prize.

At the first test séance Houdini held Margery's left hand and had his right foot pressed against her left foot. Her husband was on her other

"Margery," was controlled by holding hands with two people during a séance. But she insisted that one of those hand-holders be her husband.

side, which made Houdini suspicious. A box containing an electric bell was between Houdini's feet. It had a half-open lid that was a switch to turn on the bell when it was pressed closed. If the bell rang, could Houdini detect Margery ringing it?

After the séance Houdini said, "I've got her. All fraud. I positively felt the tendons of her leg flex and tighten as she repeatedly touched the ringing apparatus." Houdini had put a rubber bandage around his

Houdini tests out the box he designed for Margery so she couldn't pull any of her usual tricks. When she was in it, no spirits appeared.

leg just under his knee and worn it all day before the séance so that his leg would be sore and sensitive. He had rolled up his trouser so that his exposed skin was able to detect any motion Margery made as she used her foot to ring the bell. Still, one committee member was not convinced. They had another test séance. This time Margery would be encased in a cabinet, built by Houdini's cabinet maker, with only her head sticking out. During that séance, nothing even remotely psychic happened. The committee voted four to one that Margery was a fraud.

14

Houdini's Legacy

Harry Houdini died on October 31, 1926, on Halloween, as the result of an unfortunate accident. Ten days earlier, he had given a lecture exposing spiritualism at McGill University in Canada. Three students visited him in his dressing room after the performance. One of the students, a tall, strong young man, asked Houdini if it was true that he was in such good shape that he could take a blow to the stomach without any injury. Houdini was going through his mail and not really listening. He said that it was true. The young man asked if he could try to punch him and Houdini absentmindedly agreed. As he stood up, the student quickly delivered three hard blows to Houdini's abdomen before the magician had a chance to tighten his stomach muscles. Although he felt pain, he didn't realize at the time that the blows had ruptured his appendix. Infection set in, and 10 days later he was dead at the age of 52.

In spite of his very public statements that the dead cannot speak to the living, Harry Houdini had told his wife that if there was any possibility of him speaking to her from beyond the grave, he would do so. For 10 years, Bess attended séances every Halloween, listening for the code they had agreed on as proof she was hearing from him. It never came. On the tenth anniversary of her husband's death, when she did not contact

Harry's spirit, Bess declared that it was finished. The matter had been resolved once and for all.

During his lifetime, Harry Houdini was much more than an entertainer and a debunker of spiritualism. "To pull a Houdini" meant that someone made an amazing escape out of a tight spot.

Houdini spent his life constantly taking risks and challenging his fears. Perhaps his greatest fear was that he would not be remembered. He need not have worried. Ask anyone today to name the greatest magician who ever lived. Houdini still tops the list.

Houdini's funeral procession travels down Broadway in New York. The wreath at the foot of the casket was inscribed with the words "Mother Love." He was laid to rest beside his mother.

Events in the Life of Harry Houdini

March 24, 1874
Ehrich Weiss is born. (Houdini will later celebrate his birthday on April 6.)

June 22, 1894
Harry marries Bess Rahner and she takes Theo's place in the act. They become "The Houdinis."

1891
Houdini becomes a professional magician, working with Jake Hyman and later brother Theo as the "Brothers Houdini."

1887
The Weiss family settles in New York.

1895–1899
Harry and Bess tour Dime Museums while Harry develops his handcuff and straitjacket acts.

Summer, 1878
Cecilia Weiss and her sons arrive in the United States and join Rabbi Weiss in Wisconsin.

1888
Ehrich discovers Robert-Houdin's book on magic and takes the name Harry Houdini.

1900
Harry Houdini travels to Europe and becomes "The King of Handcuffs" and an international star.

October 5, 1892
On his deathbed, Rabbi Weiss asks his son always to look after his mother.

March, 1899
Harry Houdini is discovered by Martin Beck and makes the leap to vaudeville. He and Bess become top stars.

March 18, 1910
Houdini becomes
the first person
to successfully
fly an airplane
in Australia.

1902
Houdini wins a
lawsuit in Germany
over accusations
that he bribed people
to ensure his escapes.

March 17, 1904
Houdini escapes the
handcuff challenge offered
by the *Mirror*, a London
newspaper—one of his
greatest triumphs.

1913
Houdini introduces
his upside down
"Water Torture Cell"
escape. On July 13,
Cecilia Weiss dies.

1926
In August, Houdini
triumphs over Rahmen Bey.
On October 31, Houdini
dies in Detroit from an
infection due to a ruptured
appendix.

1908
Houdini introduces the
"Milk Can" escape. He also
publishes *The Unmasking
of Robert-Houdin*, a history
of magic that exposed the
tricks of his former idol.

1918
Houdini introduces
his elephant disap-
pearing act and his
walk through a wall.

1922
Houdini begins a campaign
to expose spiritualist
mediums as frauds.

1919–1922
Houdini makes
five movies and
begins his own
production
company.

1924–1925
Houdini exposes the famous
medium Margery as a fraud.

123

Bibliography

Brandon, Ruth. *The Life and Many Deaths of Harry Houdini.* New York: Random House, 1993.

Cannell, J. C. *The Secrets of Houdini.* New York: Dover Publications, Inc. 1973.

Cox, Clinton. *Houdini: Master of Illusion.* New York: Scholastic Press, 2001.

Christopher, Milbourne. *Houdini: A Pictorial Biography, Including More Than 250 Illustrations.* New York: Gramarcy Books, 1976

Gibson, Walter B. *Houdini's Escapes and Magic.* New York: Funk & Wagnalls Publishing Co., Inc. 1976.

Gibson, Walter B. & Young, Morris N. eds. *Houdini on Magic.* New York: Dover Publications, Inc., 1953.

Gresham, William Lindsay. *Houdini: The Man Who Walked Through Walls.* New York: Henry Holt and Co., 1959.

Houdini, Harry. *Miracle Mongers and Their Methods: A Complete Exposé.* Buffalo, New York: Prometheus Books, 1993.

Houdini, Harry. *The Unmasking of Robert-Houdin*: London, 1909.

Kellock, Harold. *Houdini: His Life Story.* New York: Harcourt Brace, 1928.

Lalicki, Tom. *Spellbinder: The Life of Harry Houdini.* New York: Holiday House, 2000.

Silverman, Kenneth. *Houdini!!! The Career of Erich Weiss.* New York: HarperCollins, 1996.

Sobel, Bernard. *A Pictorial History of Vaudeville.* New York: The Citadel Press, 1961.

Woog, Adam. *The Importance of Harry Houdini.* San Diego, CA: Lucent Books, 1995.

Works Cited

Note: Spelling and punctuation have been modernized for easier reading.

p. 6: "I will now perform the best escape I have ever invented." *Houdini: The Man Who Walked Through Walls* p. 150.

p. 9: "A man can only live……Music, Maestro, please!" *Houdini: The Man Who Walked Through Walls* p. 150.

p. 16: "…one morning my father awoke…" *The Importance of Harry Houdini* p. 14.

p. 25: "Shake me, I'm magic." *Houdini: A Pictorial Biography, Including More Than 250 Illustrations* Christopher, p. 13.

p. 28: "My interest in conjuring …" : Houdini, *The Unmasking of Robert-Houdin,* p.7.

p. 31: "When I clap my hands three times–behold a miracle!" *The Importance of Harry Houdini* p. 20.

p. 34: "... I contemplated quitting the show business,…." *Houdini!!! The Career of Erich Weiss.* p.20

p. 39: "I defy any manager or police official to…" *Houdini on Magic,* p. 8.

p. 40: "perhaps more in a joke than sincerity," *Houdini!!! The Career of Erich Weiss.* p. 20.

p. 41: "You can open Omaha March twenty-sixth sixty dollars…."; Human Experience: Http://www.pbs.org/wgbh/amex/houdini/peopleevents/pande01.html

p. 43: "I have spread your fame for making handcuffs….." *Houdini!!! The Career of Erich Weiss,* p32

p. 48: "I am ready to be manacled by the *Mirror* representative ..." : The Illustrated Daily Mirror, March 18, 1904: http://www.handcuffs.org/mirror/

p. 49: "Will you remove the handcuffs for a moment…" The Illustrated Daily Mirror, March 18, 1904: http://www.handcuffs.org/mirror/

p. 50: "A mighty roar of gladness…" The Illustrated Daily Mirror, March 18, 1904: http://www.handcuffs.org/mirror/

p. 51: "My brain is the key…" http://www.geocities.com/arrkagan/intro.html

p. 56: "That is not true…." *Houdini: His Life Story,* p. 141

p. 57: "The whole secret…" *Houdini's Escapes and Magic,* p. 24.

p. 58: "He mingles among the committee…" *Houdini!!! The Career of Erich Weiss,* p. 54

p. 60-61: "I saw a maniac struggling…" *Houdini on Magic,* p. 9

p. 62: "Most of my success in Europe…" *Houdini!!! The Career of Erich Weiss* Silverman, p. 51